AF521841

Liz Carpenter

Liz Carpenter, 1967.

Liz Carpenter

Girl from Salado

Betty Wilke Cox

EAKIN PRESS ★ Austin, Texas

FIRST EDITION

Published in the United States of America
By Eakin Press
An Imprint of Sunbelt Media, Inc.
P.O. Drawer 90159 ★ Austin, TX 78709-0159

ISBN 0-89015-940-8

Dedicated to the daughters
and granddaughters
of the Women's Movement.

Young woman in Washington.
— Photo by Hessler Portraits, Washington, D.C.

Contents

Liz Carpenter and the author examine one of Liz's many scrapbooks of clippings and photos from her Washington years. (Photo by Paula Stout)

Preface

I spent the summer of 1990 living in the guest house of Grass Roots, housesitting Liz Carpenter's home in the hills west of Austin. For three wonderful months I ate peaches from the LBJ Ranch, read stacks of books from the Howson Branch of the Austin Public Library, and took walks alongside the winding Skyline Drive and Wildcat Hollow.

Each morning the deer woke me, demanding that I get up and throw corn out for them. Each night marauding raccoons rambled past the patio door. From the hillside I watched the jeweled night skyline of the capital city, Fourth of July fireworks, and fierce lightning storms.

I read *Getting Better All the Time* while sitting where I could look up and see scenes that Liz describes in her opening chapters.

When Liz came home, she and I were together in her office, trying — against deadline — to get one of her many magazine articles ready to mail. We passed the pages back and forth, commenting, correcting, making each other laugh.

In an offhanded way, not looking up from the manuscript, Liz asked, "How would you like to work for me a couple of days a week?"

Talk about an offer you can't refuse!

I continued my full-time job as a librarian in the editorial library of the *Austin American-Statesman* and worked with Liz in her home office when I could. I soon learned how much we had in common. We were born in the same decade, the 1920s, and grew up during the Great Depression. We were proud of our Texas heritage. For twelve years of our lives Franklin Roosevelt was *the* president. We were cub reporters during World War II.

I can't say just when I began thinking of writing her biography, but the events of September 1991 gave me the push I needed. I outlined my idea to Ed Eakin, publisher, and received a prompt acceptance.

Liz was pleased, I think, with the idea that her children, Scott and Christy, her grandson, Les Carpenter, her step-granddaughter, Bonnie Bizzell, and all her nieces and nephews and cousins would be able to read her life story. She made family records available to me. She gave me the names of friends, many of whom have known her since childhood. Busy as she was with her own writing and speaking engagements, she'd take a minute to swivel her chair around and say, "Ask me something."

I'd grab a notebook. "Tell me about the little yellow dog," I'd say. Or, "Did you *really* bring a Black Angus calf up on the stage?" Or the question I hated to ask: "Where were you when you heard the shots?"

I hope you will enjoy reading about this remarkable woman, and that you will find her life's story as inspiring as I have.

Acknowledgments

Both as writer and librarian, I gratefully acknowledge the staff and resources of the following: Austin History Center, Austin Public Library, Barker Texas History Center (now the Center for American History), Bell County Museum, Belton Public Library, Cleburne Public Library, Layland Museum, LBJ School of Public Affairs Library, Lyndon B. Johnson Library, Perry Casteneda Library, Texas State Library, University of Texas Ex-Students' Association, University of Texas News and Information Service, and University of Texas Medical Branch at Galveston.

These people, many of them family or friends of Liz Carpenter, graciously gave their time, patiently answered questions, and encouraged me along the way: Claudia Anderson, Lena Armstrong, Mary Love Bailey, Maggie Balough, Carol Barrett, Jean Begeman Bergmark, Bonnie Bizzell, Erma Bombeck, Inci A. Bowman, Martha Boyd, Christy Carpenter, Jean and Scott Carpenter and their son Les, Alicia A. Cox, Patti Nolen Crain, Bill Cryer, Anita Davis, Marshall DeBruhl, Sue Kone Drake, Ralph Elder, Creekmore Fath, Allen Fisher, Betty Friedan, Jacque Goettsche, Michael R. Green, Coleen and Dick Hardin, Carol Sutherland Hatfield, Kay Head, Lorraine Barnes Hood, Tina Houston, Henrietta Jacobsen, Lee Kelly, Dorcas Larrabee, Chuck McCarthy, Malcolm McLean, Maxine Mesinger, Homer Olsen, Billy Porterfield, Nan Robertson, Eugenia Worley Schock,

Jewel Scott, Michele Stanush, Doreen Stevens, George and Jean Sutherland, Kay Sutherland, Mabel Sutherland, Betty Talmadge, Ruthe L. Winegarten, Anita and Eugene Wukasch, and Linda Zezulka.

My research assistants have proved invaluable. Kristen Depowski started me off with searches of electronic databases, examination of resources, and interviews with Liz Carpenter's childhood friends. Kris has a master's degree in communications from the University of Texas. Christian Gonzalez ferreted out books on Mrs. Roosevelt's "press girls." Christian also came up with a musician's description of *Ruffles and Flourishes.* He is now an intern with the Hispanic Link News Service in Washington, D.C. Helen Lang came to my rescue in the last few months, bringing intelligence, energy, and enthusiasm as she learned the skills of library research.

I am personally indebted to the following:

Shirley James, for her memory and for the facts at her fingertips.

Dr. Ronald K. DeFord and Mrs. Marion W. DeFord, for friendship, an atmosphere of scholarship, and the resources of their private library.

John H. and Maren Hicks, my good neighbors, for doing anything they could to help me stick with this project.

Terry and Alice Curtis and their children, Colette, Kevin, and Kristi, for friendship, encouragement, and helping me keep my ducks in a row. When my old word processor crunched the first hundred pages of this manuscript, Terry rushed to my rescue with a "loaner" until I was able to get a new one.

Linda A. Cox, my daughter-in-law, for her keen eyes and insightful questions and especially for her invaluable assistance with the last chapter, "Calling All Women." Linda attended First Lady Hillary Rodham Clinton's talk in Austin. She shared her impressions with me, and gave me the wonderful quote from Bill Moyers with which I close the book.

Mike Cox, my son, a writer and knowledgeable bookman, for always encouraging me. He read and commented on some of the earlier chapters as I was feeling my way along for form and content. He suggested reference books for further research and was often able to lend them to me from his extensive private collection. He was patient with innumerable phone calls that began, "Do you have just a minute for me to read this page to you?" In 1993 he was inducted into the Texas Institute of Letters.

Vice President Lyndon B. Johnson (left) and President John F. Kennedy with Liz Carpenter.

Prologue: That Day in Dallas

Friday, November 22, 1963, began with a gray drizzle.

Thousands of people lined the Dallas parade route, waiting to catch a glimpse of the handsome young president and his glamorous wife. Many people cheered and waved signs of greeting.

Staff members and reporters on the motorcade press bus talked and laughed as they discussed President John F. Kennedy's successful visits the day before to San Antonio, Houston, and Fort Worth. They looked forward to that night's scheduled barbecue at the LBJ Ranch near Stonewall. This was the first trip to Texas for many of the people on the press bus.

Liz Carpenter, executive assistant to Vice President Lyndon B. Johnson, helped welcome them to her home state. Liz visited briefly with first one, then another. She passed out press kits for the reporters. She kept the men and women laughing with her blend of facts and funny stories about Texas and politics.

Suddenly, Liz heard three small sounds: *Ping. Ping,*

ping. They sounded like firecrackers. *A prank,* she thought.

She looked out the window of the bus. Escort motorcyclists had turned around. Two policemen were running up a grassy slope. That was not unusual, Liz knew. Many policemen surround a presidential motorcade route.

The bus sped up and soon arrived at the Dallas Trade Mart. Earlier, more than 2,000 people had gathered inside the Trade Mart, waiting to greet President and Mrs. Kennedy, Vice President and Mrs. Johnson, Texas Governor John B. Connally and Mrs. Connally, and other officials.

As soon as Liz stepped down from the bus, she realized that something had gone terribly wrong. Where was the rest of the motorcade? Where were the people waiting for the president? Where was the vice president?

In her haste Liz left her straw tote bag on the bus. The bag contained that day's *Dallas Morning News* and the extra press kits.

Liz walked toward the Trade Mart entrance with Evelyn Lincoln, the president's personal secretary, Marie Fehmer, the vice president's personal secretary, and Jack Valenti, a public relations man from Houston. A policeman stopped them.

"You can't go in," the officer said. "Everyone's been sent home."

But Liz could still see people milling around, puzzled. Then she saw a Secret Service agent using an outside pay phone near the door.

Evelyn Lincoln hurried over and spoke briefly to him. As Mrs. Lincoln returned, Liz saw that her face was ashen. She looked stricken.

"The president has been shot," she told them. "I must get to Mrs. Kennedy."

Marie Fehmer cried out. She covered her face with her hands.

All of the orderly plans for the president's visit to Dallas fell apart. The people who had gathered at the

Trade Mart for the luncheon and President Kennedy's appearance had been told about the assassination. There would be no luncheon. Everyone was leaving. Some followed the news on their transistor radios. Many wandered around in shock and confusion.

The motorcade bus had left Liz and her companions stranded.

Liz rushed toward the parking lot, searching for anyone who could help them. She saw a parked car. A man and a woman were sitting in the front seat. Liz beat against the closed window and cried out for help. The couple didn't even look at her. They appeared to be in shock. Perhaps they had just heard of the shooting on their car radio.

Then Liz spotted another car, which looked like an unmarked police car. She ran to it just as the driver was getting out.

"These people are on the president's staff," she said. "You've got to get them to the hospital!"

The off-duty law enforcement officer nodded. "I'll have to get this stuff out of the back seat first," he said.

Impatiently, Liz grabbed dry cleaning and bundles of laundry from the car. She helped the officer stow them in the trunk.

Dallas traffic was hopelessly snarled. People and cars that had lined the parade route now choked the streets. Liz was grateful for their driver's skill. He drove over curbs and cut across grass to get them to the hospital.

Crowded with the others in the back seat, Marie Fehmer clutched her rosary and prayed.

"It can't be true," Liz tried to reassure herself and the others. "It's just a rumor. You all know how these things get started."

There was only one telephone at the rear entrance to Parkland Hospital. News reporters were searching for additional phones so they could phone in their stories.

Liz saw the president's limousine convertible, Mrs. Kennedy's spray of red roses, and a pool of blood beside the car.

It is true, Liz realized. Even then, it was too terrible to believe.

Evelyn Lincoln went immediately to find Mrs. Kennedy. Soon Mrs. Lincoln returned to the anxious group.

"They've sent for a priest," she told them.

John Kennedy was the first Catholic president of the United States. A priest was summoned to perform the last rites of the church.

Liz and Marie Fehmer wanted to find Vice President Johnson as quickly as possible. Officials took them and several other staff members to private rooms in the administrative area of the hospital. From there Liz was unable to hear the page over the public address system calling her to come to Johnson.

Governor Connally also had been seriously — perhaps fatally — wounded, they learned. Doctors were treating him in a room near where the president lay.

A thousand thoughts raged through Liz's mind. Paramount was the question: Where's the vice president? As far as anyone knew, Johnson had not been injured. Where could he be?

"Maybe he's still at the Trade Mart," someone suggested.

Liz and Marie Fehmer hurried back there to look for him. Although the sun had come out, it did little to lift their spirits.

The two women found no trace of Johnson at the Trade Mart. Again they flagged a police car and rushed back to Parkland Hospital.

Liz got there just in time. Lyndon and Lady Bird Johnson, surrounded by Secret Service agents and several Texas congressmen, pulled out of the hospital driveway in unmarked cars. As the cars drove away, Liz saw Mrs. Johnson gesture to her: *Follow us!*

Liz's police driver made a quick turn. They headed for Love Field. *Air Force One,* the president's plane, was waiting there to take the official group back to Washington.

As the cars sped across Dallas, at about 1:30, the radio news confirmed everyone's worst fears.

President Kennedy was dead.

Liz, a journalist for many years before joining Johnson's staff, knew he would need a statement for the press when he arrived in Washington.

Through eyes brimmed with tears, Liz fumbled in her purse for something to write on. All she could find were a handful of Lady Bird Johnson's cards — small, white cards decorated with little gold birds. Mrs. Johnson used the cards when people asked for her autograph. On the backs of those cards Liz wrote fifty-eight words. The words just seemed to come to her.

When Liz reached the waiting airplane, government officials quickly hustled her aboard. People who had been talking and laughing only a few hours earlier were silent and sad. Liz heard someone sobbing.

Seated next to four pool reporters, Liz block-printed the fifty-eight words on a handful of three-by-five cards. She handed them to Bill Moyers, at that time deputy director of the Peace Corps, who took them to the rear cabin. In a few minutes Moyers returned and asked Liz to come to the cabin Johnson was using as an office.

Johnson made several phone calls from the plane. He phoned the late president's mother, Mrs. Rose Kennedy. He and Mrs. Johnson offered what words of sympathy they could.

Liz and other staff members helped with the necessary work. They also tried to console one another.

Johnson sent for Judge Sarah T. Hughes to administer the oath of office. Just two years earlier, in October 1961, President Kennedy had appointed her to the U.S. District Court in Dallas. Judge Hughes was the first woman appointed as a federal judge in Texas. The sixty-seven-year-old judge was prominent in her profession. She was one of the few strong women speaking out for women's rights.

As Judge Hughes boarded the plane, everyone gathered in the front cabin to watch the swearing-in ceremony. Some of the people on the plane, aware of the historic nature of the event, crowded up close.

Liz remained in the background. In addition to her sadness, she felt a deep sense of shame — shame for her country and for her beloved Texas — that a president of the United States had been shot and killed on the streets of Dallas.

Judge Hughes was a petite woman, not even as tall as Liz's own height of five feet, one inch. She appeared even smaller as she embraced Lyndon and Lady Bird, whom she had known for many years.

Someone picked up a Catholic missal from President Kennedy's cabin and handed it to Judge Hughes. "This is a Catholic Bible," he told the judge.

Johnson placed his left hand on the book. He raised his right hand and repeated the brief oath of office. His wife, Lady Bird, was at his side. Mrs. Kennedy stood on the other side.

From where she was standing, Liz could hear Judge Hughes' voice shaking as she administered the oath.

Lyndon B. Johnson was now the thirty-sixth president of the United States.

"Let's get this plane in the air," he said.

Liz had the feeling that he was in control. She comforted herself with the thought that through this whole terrible ordeal the United States had never been without a leader. At each step, she thought, Johnson had done everything necessary for the security of the nation.

Liz and the Johnsons had been close friends for almost twenty years. Liz realized with a jolt she would never again feel comfortable calling them Lyndon and Lady Bird. From now on, it would be President and Mrs. Johnson.

Liz's seat on *Air Force One* was across the aisle from the grieving Kennedy staff. She longed to reach out with some word of comfort. What could she possibly say?

Air Force One landed at Andrews Air Force Base, Maryland, near Washington, D.C. A silent group of officials and journalists waited. A chill wind whipped through the evening air.

President Johnson faced the television cameras and spoke the solemn words Liz Carpenter had written for him:

> "This is a sad time for all people. We have suffered a loss that cannot be weighed. For me, it is a deep personal tragedy. I know that the world shares the sorrow that Mrs. Kennedy and her family bear. I will do my best. That is all I can do. I ask for your help — and God's."

President and Mrs. Johnson and Liz flew by presidential helicopter from Andrews to the lawn of the White House. The tall new president from Texas leaned down to speak softly to his executive assistant.

"Liz, you go with Lady Bird," he said. "Help her all you can."

President Johnson turned and walked briskly toward his office in the Executive Office building. He had been in touch with his advisers by phone from aboard *Air Force One*. A number of meetings already had been scheduled.

Secret Service agents drove Mrs. Johnson and Liz in the vice-presidential limousine to The Elms, the Johnsons' residence in Washington.

Luci, the Johnsons' youngest daughter, met them at the door and embraced her mother.

Liz telephoned her children right away to let them know she was back in Washington. She knew they would have many questions to ask about President Kennedy's assassination. She wanted to comfort and reassure them.

Her seventeen-year-old son, Scott, was a twelfth-grade student at Woodrow Wilson High School.

"I was driving back from taking Daddy to the airport when I heard the news on the car radio," Scott told her. "Mom, they said the motorcade was sprayed with bullets. I didn't know if you were alive or . . ." His voice broke.

Liz was stunned. Caught up in the nation's concerns, she had never thought her family might be worried about her own safety.

“School let out and I went to St. Alban’s,” Scott added. St. Alban’s Episcopal Church, on the grounds of the National Cathedral, was the Carpenters’ family church.

Christy, Liz’s thirteen-year-old daughter, was a ninth-grade student at Holton Arms. She had gone to another church with her classmates, she told her mother.

The tragic news of President Kennedy’s assassination spread rapidly. People all over the United States gathered in solemn prayer services at their churches. In years to come they would remember exactly where they were and what they were doing when they heard of the president’s death in Dallas.

Liz rejoined Mrs. Johnson in the living room of The Elms.

Mrs. Johnson and Liz sat and talked quietly. The household staff prepared food and set it out in the dining room. Although they had scarcely eaten all day, neither woman was hungry.

Secret Service agents stationed themselves around the house. Although it was well after dark and the gates to the property were locked, newspaper and television reporters gathered outside The Elms. Television spotlights focused on the home of the new president.

“Let me go down to the gate and give them a statement,” Liz said. “They won’t go away until we do.”

“I can’t make a statement, Liz. Not yet.” Mrs. Johnson murmured. She was not eager to step into her new role as First Lady. “It’s all been a dreadful nightmare, but we must find the strength to go on.”

Liz quickly jotted down the last few words. “That’s perfect,” she said. “That’s all you need to say.”

Liz gave Mrs. Johnson’s statement to the waiting reporters. Many of them were her friends and former colleagues. Tonight there was no joking and laughing among them.

The Kennedy years had been filled with such hope, such optimism. As she left The Elms to return to her husband, Les, her two children, and her own home at 4701

Woodway Lane, Liz knew that on this day her life — and that of every American — had changed forever.

Liz Carpenter was prepared for what was to come. She knew how to meet challenges and face adversity. It was in her blood . . .

1. Brush Country Bride

Mary E was alone in the cabin. A ruckus from the hen house waked her. She peered out into the darkness. Strain as she might, all she could see were a pair of eyes gleaming back at her.

She fired one shot and went back to bed.

The next morning she dressed hastily and went out to the hen house to investigate.

Mary E had killed a skunk. Not only killed it, but shot it right between the eyes.

Mary and her husband, Tom, had few neighbors in the sparsely settled range country of South Texas, but word spread among them faster than a prairie fire. Mary E's stock went up considerably with the hardy ranching folk. Maybe she wasn't just a helpless Southern belle after all.

Mary Elizabeth Robertson and Thomas Shelton Sutherland III were the same age, both born in June 1887. Both had been students at Thomas Arnold High School in Salado, Texas. Both had attended the Methodist Church.

Mary E's charms had captivated Tom, and he had asked a friend to introduce them formally. Only then did he begin his courtship.

Tom was tall and good-looking, as the Sutherland men tended to be. Mary E was described by her many admirers as "a dark-eyed beauty."

The couple had married November 2, 1910, in the Robertson home in Salado. Then Tom took his Bell County bride to Nueces Canyon in the untamed brush country of South Texas.

Maclin Robertson had given his daughter his own favorite Colt revolver to take with her. A strange wedding present, but one that definitely came in handy.

Ranch life carried many hardships for Mary E. She had moved from the spacious, twenty-four-room Robertson place in Salado to little more than a one-room shack on the Raney Ranch in the brush country. She had grown up in a large family — three brothers, three sisters, and dozens of cousins.

Now she found herself alone for days at a time while her young husband worked as a stockman. She took comfort from the precious books she had brought with her from the Robertson library. And she took comfort from her father's Colt revolver.

On September 21, 1911, it was time for Mary E to deliver her first child. Her pregnancy was not going well.

Tom made his wife as comfortable as possible in the back of a wagon and made the tiring thirty-mile journey to Uvalde. He found room and board for Mary E at a dollar a day and arranged for a doctor to attend her.

After an exhausting twelve-hour labor, Mary E delivered her baby. She waited in vain for the reassurance of the first cry. The infant had been born nearly lifeless.

Quickly, the doctor dunked the small body into basins of water — first warm, then cold — in an effort to shock air into its lungs. Finally he pronounced the infant out of danger and handed him to his anxious mother. The boy was named Thomas Shelton Sutherland IV, after his father, of course. They would often call him "Son," following the custom of the first-born male child.

After Mary E had several weeks to convalesce from the difficult birth, Tom came to Uvalde to take her and their first child back to the Raney Ranch.

Mary E was no longer alone. Before Tommy was toddling, his mother began reading to him, sharing her love for fine literature. As she read to him from the works of Byron, Keats, and Shelley, Tommy absorbed the rhythm and cadence of the British poets.

Ranch life suited Tom Sutherland like a pair of comfortable well-worn boots. He had been born to it. His father, Thomas Shelton Sutherland II, and his mother, Laura Lizzie Rogers Sutherland, lived nearby with eleven of their children.

Tom spoke Spanish well and enjoyed the company of the Mexican ranch hands. He also loved good horses. When Tommy was old enough, Tom lifted his son up into the saddle with him. They rode together through the brush, often flushing a rush of whitewing doves, sometimes spotting deer and wild turkey.

In the spring of the year, fragrant yellow blossoms of huisache, mesquite, and prickly pear washed the brush country with deceptive beauty. Any time of the year thorns and twisted, stunted branches snatched the rider's clothing, punished his horse's flanks, and shielded stray cattle from sight for weeks at a stretch. In most places, the brush was so dense a man might have to search the horizon for a windmill or water tower to get his bearings.

This wild country was dear and familiar to the Sutherlands. The first of the Sutherland family, or clan, came from Scotland to America in the early colonial days and eventually settled in Alabama. George Sutherland, with his brother-in-law, Jesse White, and a group called the "Alabama Settlement," arrived in Texas in 1830. The group joined Stephen F. Austin's colony.

In 1836, when Texas fought for independence from

the Republic of Mexico, George Sutherland commanded a company of volunteers at San Antonio and at San Jacinto. His son, seventeen-year-old William, died at the Alamo.

General Sam Houston realized the Mexican forces outnumbered his small army. After the fall of the Alamo at San Antonio, he reluctantly ordered a retreat from the settlement at Gonzales. He led his ragtag troops toward the San Jacinto River.

The Sutherland family tells the story that George Sutherland, grieving the death of his young son, confronted General Houston. He insisted that Houston stop retreating. "Stand and fight!" he demanded. Whether this encounter actually took place, the story reflects the fierce patriotism of the Sutherland clan.

In 1913 both Sutherland families — parents and grandparents — lived in Harlingen in the Rio Grande Valley for a while. Tommy was never a lonely child. He grew up with grandparents, four Sutherland aunts almost his own age — Mable, Ara, Emma Jean, and Lucille — and numerous other aunts and uncles.

Tom, his younger brother Wells, and their father rode from ranch to ranch. They bought calves to feed, fatten, and ship to the Kansas City stockyards.

One day Tommy was riding in an open buggy with his Grandfather Sutherland. He saw a strange contraption.

"Look, Grandpapa!" he exclaimed.

It was a buggy, just like theirs, but the driver had no horse. Tommy had seen his first automobile. Not too long after that, Tommy rode in a "horseless carriage," or "gas buggy," as some people called the early automobiles.

Tom, Mary E, and Tommy moved from Harlingen in the Rio Grande Valley to Georgetown. They were going to stay with Mary E's relatives, the Robertson family. The journey in a Model T Ford covered some 330 miles of mostly unpaved road.

As the family crossed the sprawling King Ranch, the narrow wheels of the Model T managed to dig themselves into the loose, sandy soil. Several Mexican cowboys from the King Ranch had a good laugh at this sorry spectacle. They spun their leather lariats, lassoed the automobile as they would have a cantankerous steer, and pulled it free.

The Maclin Robertsons had taken a house in Georgetown so that their children could attend Southwestern University there. Tommy was happy playing with his mother's younger brother, Gordon Robertson. Although the family took good care of him, Tommy began to miss his mother and wondered why he didn't see her.

"Where's Mama?" he kept asking.

Finally, on June 26, 1914, his father led him into his mother's bedroom. Mary E showed Tommy his new baby sister, Alice. She had been named for Mary E's mother, Alice Josephine Woods Robertson.

"What do you think of her, Son?" his mother asked.

"She looks like a little mouse," Tommy blurted. He knew immediately this wasn't the answer his parents had hoped for. He promised himself he would do better next time.

The family left Georgetown and stayed at the Robertson home in Salado, where Tom and Mary E had married almost four years earlier. There Tommy began to get acquainted with his mother's family.

He watched his grandfather, Maclin Robertson, as though trying to memorize every detail. Robertson was silver-haired and wore a big mustache. He always dressed like a Southern gentleman in a long, pearl-gray coat. He usually sat astride his favorite horse, a big bay named Hal.

One day Robertson noticed the small, silent child who had been studying him so closely. He urged Hal closer.

"Want to ride out to the pasture?" he asked. "Reach up your hand."

Tommy was speechless. It was the first time he could remember that Grandpapa Robertson had spoken to him. Before Tommy could think of a suitable reply, Robertson leaned down from his saddle. He scooped the child up and rode off.

It was a good thing that Tommy had learned to ride with his father, or he surely would have fallen off. Tommy had acquired a deep love of horses that would last all his life.

Tom and Mary E, with their children Tommy and Alice, settled on a small farm near Salado. The children rode horseback to Salado to attend school.

Tom's parents, Tom and Laura Lizzie, and six of their younger children, had moved up from Harlingen and were living on a ranch near Florence. The family called the place Hog Mountain Ranch, named for the highest peak in Bell County. The Sutherlands had a good-sized vegetable garden, and wild plums grew along Rocky Creek.

In the lingering heat of the first day of September, 1920, Mary E smiled her familiar gentle smile and pulled back one corner of the coverlet to show another new baby to her son.

Tommy stared down at the tiny red, wrinkled face. This baby sister, as far as he could tell, was no great improvement over his sister Alice, born six years ago. He had blundered rather badly that time. Now Tommy, just three weeks shy of his ninth birthday, was mature enough to realize that grownups expected a certain amount of oohing and cooing as a matter of courtesy.

Tom Sutherland regarded his wife and new baby with pride and with relief. Mary E never had an easy time with childbirth. But giving birth here in the Robertson house in Salado, with her mother and her sisters to assist and comfort her, was a far cry from Tommy's birth in Uvalde.

This child, nestled in the crook of her arm, Mary E would name for her grandmother, Mary Elizabeth Robertson, and for herself. The girl's name would be Mary Elizabeth Sutherland. In later years she would be known as Liz.

Tom could hardly wait to ride the ten miles over to Hog Mountain Ranch and share the good news with his parents and brothers and sisters.

2. Cotton, Cattle, and Calamity

Mary Elizabeth's father viewed the future with optimism.

"Automobiles are changing everything," he told his wife enthusiastically.

Mary E smiled at her husband as she tended their new baby. Full of energy and ambition, Tom Sutherland couldn't be still a minute.

"Builders can't keep up with the demand for paved roads," he continued. He paced restlessly in the kitchen of their farm home near Salado.

He was right about roads. He couldn't foresee the natural disaster that would change the course of all their lives within the year.

Roads often were not much more than tracks and ruts in Texas' earlier years. Each county was responsible for the building and upkeep of roads within its boundaries. As more and more Texans bought "Tin Lizzies," drivers demanded hard-topped roads and safe highway bridges.

The legislature had established the Texas Highway

Department in 1917. A few years later, the Highway Department took over responsibility for a statewide highway system. Now contractors were building new roads everywhere.

Tom went to the nearest road crew and asked for a job. The boss hired him on the spot.

The Sutherland men all seemed cut from the same pattern. Tom was tall, strong, and a hard worker. He spoke Spanish well from his years in South Texas. He relayed work orders to the Mexican laborers.

He quickly rose to foreman and began to dream of owning his own construction business.

Papa Sutherland had told his son there was no longer any money in the cattle business. He was right.

The cattle operation had been profitable enough during World War I and for two or three years following. People were glad to be free of wartime rationing. They were willing to pay a good price for meat. But then a drought drove beef prices up. In 1920 the value of beef cattle dropped.

"You can't *give* them away," stockmen told each other sadly.

Papa Sutherland had a load of cattle on the train bound for Kansas City when the market fell. He couldn't sell them. He still owed money to the ranchers from whom he had bought them. He owed the bank and the railroad.

"What will you do, Papa?" Tom asked his father.

"I've got no choice," Papa Sutherland replied. He began selling off his land to pay his debts.

The family had made the long move from South Texas partly to provide good schools for their children. Hog Mountain Ranch, near Florence, was the last piece of property Tom and Laura Lizzie owned.

The collapse of the cattle market hurt many people. Banks began calling in their loans. Cattlemen, prosperous only a few years before, now faced bankruptcy. The First State Bank in Salado, open since 1911, closed its doors in 1920. A number of other businesses in Salado closed that year, leaving empty buildings on both sides of the main street.

As businesses failed and farm prices fell, many people moved from Salado to larger towns — Belton, Temple, or Killeen. As families left, schools could no longer offer the best education for the few children who remained.

Papa Sutherland's children were riding horseback to attend a one-room country school about two and a half miles from Hog Mountain Ranch. Tom and Mary E's children, Tommy and Alice, rode from the farm into Salado to go to school. They were all bright children, eager to learn. The Sutherlands were not sure their children were getting the education they deserved.

Mary Elizabeth's first birthday, September 1, 1921, dawned clear, hot, and dry. Tom and Mary E watched the weather with concern. They feared a prolonged drought such as the one in 1918 and 1919. Rain hadn't fallen in two months. Cotton bolls weren't filling out.

The scarce crop drove prices up. When the cotton market opened after Labor Day, prices were up a bit more. That was cheering news for farmers, but only if they could pick a good crop, bale it, and get the bales to the gin.

A slow drizzle began in midafternoon on Thursday, September 8.

"Not a drought-breaker yet," folks said. "If it just keeps up . . ."

The rain kept up, growing in intensity toward evening. By Friday morning — a dull, gray day — rain fell steadily and showed no sign of quitting.

A cloudburst, pushed into Central Texas by a tropical storm in the Gulf of Mexico, dropped inches of rain in minutes. Swollen creeks and rivers washed out roads, swept away bridges, and damaged railroad trestles. Tornadoes spawned by the violent weather destroyed homes, barns, and cotton gins.

Mary E, with Tommy, Alice, and the one-year-old baby, Mary Elizabeth, sought the shelter of the high ground at the Robertson plantation home.

Not until the following Sunday, September 11, did most people learn of the full severity of the storm that had swept over them. In some areas, up to fourteen inches of rain had fallen in a few hours. Perhaps as many as 600 Central Texans died. Most of them drowned in the surging, muddy waters. It was the worst flood since 1913, everyone said.

First the cattle market had collapsed. Now almost everything the two Sutherland families owned was gone or badly damaged. Clearly, the time had come to make a change. They did what so many other rural Texans did in the 1920s. They moved to town.

The families rented a large house in Belton. Papa Tom, Laura Lizzie, and six of their children still at home — the four girls, Mabel, Ara, Emma Jean, and Lucille, and the two boys, Wills and Frank — lived on the first floor. Tom and Mary E, with Tommy, Alice, and the baby, Mary Elizabeth, lived upstairs. Except for the leaky roof, it was a comfortable enough arrangement.

As soon as he could find a buyer, Papa Sutherland sold the Hog Mountain Ranch. He drove his few remaining head of cattle to a feedlot in town. He fed them cottonseed cake from the Belton cottonseed mill.

Mary Elizabeth perched beside Papa, as she called her Grandfather Sutherland, on the wooden seat of the spring wagon. Little more than a toddler, she squealed with delight as Papa snapped the leather reins and urged the horse to giddyap.

"Giddyap!" she echoed.

Papa was glad to have his fourteen-month-old grandchild with him on the trips to the mill and to the feedlot. Mary Elizabeth's constant chatter and her bright-eyed attention to everything went a long way toward turning a dreary chore into a pleasant jaunt.

Road construction workers were needed more than

ever after the damaging flood. Tom had no trouble finding jobs. He often had to be away from home for weeks at a time. When he came home, he had money to pay the bills, extra food for the table, and sometimes small treats for the children.

Just as Mary E bent to take a pan of cornbread from the oven, Tom might burst through the door. His presence filled the house with energy and good humor.

"Set those beans aside, Mary E," he would say. "Tonight we eat *steak*!"

Depending on where he had been working, Tom brought other delicacies, such as juicy cantaloupe from the Pecos country or fresh oysters from the Texas coast. He could whip up a kettle of oyster stew with rich milk, globs of melting butter, and a generous sprinkling of black pepper on top. His homecomings were always cause for celebration.

Papa Sutherland's health began to fail. Born February 27, 1861, just before the Civil War began, he was growing old. A man of the saddle, always robust and healthy, he tired easily now. He felt less able to make his rounds and tend to his business affairs.

One of his grown daughters, Minnie Bell (Mrs. Aulsey Anderson), moved to Belton from Brownsville to take care of her father and help her mother, Laura Lizzie, with the younger children. Minnie Bell stayed upstairs with Mary E. One glance at her sister-in-law's full figure told Minnie Bell another Sutherland was on the way.

Papa died May 3, 1923. The next day Mary E was in labor with her fourth child. She named the baby George (Robertson) Sutherland IX. She chose the name George to honor the Sutherland who had led the family to Texas almost a hundred years before, and others of that name dating back to the Scottish clans.

Mary E had grown accustomed to her husband's absences when the couple lived in the South Texas brush country. Then she had had only her baby son Tommy and her treasured books to keep her company. Now she had no time to be lonely — or even to enjoy a little solitude. She had four children: twelve-year-old Tommy, nine-year-old Alice, two-year-old Mary Elizabeth, and baby George.

Equally comforting, Mary E's sister, Gladys, lived only a few streets away. Gladys, now Mrs. Duncan McLean, had children of her own. One son, Malcolm, was a little younger than Tommy. Another son, Douglas Keith, was a scant month older than baby George. Gladys also had a daughter, Gladyne. Another of Mary E's sisters, Birdie, now Mrs. Jefferson Davis Howell, also lived in Belton for a time.

Little Mary Elizabeth never lacked attention and companionship. There were always her brothers and sister, her young Sutherland aunts and uncles, her Robertson cousins.

And in the summer, there was Salado.

3. Salado Summers

Three-year-old Mary Elizabeth stretched out her arms to her father. "Lift me up, Daddy," she said. "Lift me up."

Tom Sutherland swept his daughter up and seated her behind the saddle of Grandfather Robertson. Mary Elizabeth wrapped her arms as far around Maclin Robertson's waist as she could reach. She held on tightly as he rode his big bay horse, Hal, around the Salado farm.

Summers in Salado were special times for the children. Tommy was old enough to work on road construction crews with his father. Alice shared household duties with her mother and her aunts. But there was always the lure of the "Blue Hole," a favorite swimming spot. There were horses to ride and trees to climb, picnics with frozen custard from the wooden churn packed with ice and coarse salt, socials and hymn-singing at the Methodist Church. Dozens of visiting cousins spread sleeping pallets, placed to catch the night's cooling breezes, in the halls of the Robertson home.

Young Mary Elizabeth was free to discover the delights of the rambling antebellum plantation-style house, the pecan and oak tree-shaded yard, and the clear Salado Creek that sliced through the pastures. And she loved riding behind her grandfather.

Maclin Robertson silently lowered his grandchild to the ground. He rode off to put Hal in the stable. Mary Elizabeth hurried along the walkway lined with twelve arborvitae, six on each side. They were named for the apostles. Matthew, Mark, Luke, John — Mary Elizabeth knew each one. She bounded across the wide veranda and flung open the door.

As she entered the house she heard laughter. A tantalizing chocolatey smell was wafting down the long hall from the kitchen. Aunt Gladys and Aunt Birdie were making fudge.

Mary Elizabeth scurried past the front parlor with an uneasy glance over her shoulder. The parlor was a lovely place at night. The glow of lamplight chased the scary shadows from every corner. The room filled with laughter and conversation. But during the daytime, shutters and heavy drapes shut out the sun's heat. Enough daylight seeped in for Mary Elizabeth to see the large oil paintings. Several generations of her stern-faced ancestors hung in solemn rows.

The gloomy room with its dark portraits of long-departed kinfolk frightened the small child. She never willingly went into the parlor alone.

"Remember who you are," Mary E told her children. Mary E wanted them to know their heritage. The children grew up knowing many details of their Robertson and Sutherland ancestors. To these two large old families, Texas history was never merely long-ago dates and half-forgotten names. It was real and familiar.

Mary E's family, the Robertsons, had come to America from Scotland. They settled in Virginia and Tennessee during the American colonial days. In 1823 Sterling Clack Robertson came to Texas with a group of friends and business associates. They hunted and explored the area around the Brazos River. When the other men returned to Tennessee, Robertson remained in Texas. He visited the new settlement of American colonists at San Felipe.

What he saw impressed Robertson. He decided to return home and persuade other Americans to come to Texas. He formed the Nashville Company, named for the city in Tennessee his father had helped found.

Texas belonged to the Republic of Mexico. In 1825, Robertson received permission from the Mexican government to bring as many as 800 families from Tennessee and other southern states to help colonize Texas. Only Stephen F. Austin's grant was larger. These *empresarios* obtained grants of land from the Mexican government in return for establishing colonies.

Sterling Robertson's son, Elijah, was just a lad when he first traveled with his father on horseback from Tennessee to Texas. He went to school in San Antonio, then a small Mexican town, to learn the Spanish language.

As a child Mary Elizabeth often heard a story handed down in the family. The story told how her ancestor got his name. Elijah originally was named for his father, Sterling C. Robertson. The boy's Catholic teachers in San Antonio insisted he must have a "Christian" (that is, biblical) name. According to the story, he added "Elijah," the name of his grandfather. In later life Elijah signed his name as E. Sterling C. Robertson.

After two years of intensive study in San Antonio, Elijah was able to help translate the land grants and other legal documents issued by the Mexican officials.

The colonists from the United States soon found themselves in disagreement with the Mexican government. The Americans believed many of the laws were harsh and hard to obey. The Mexicans feared the American settlers would soon outnumber them.

Robertson, like Austin, made several trips south of the Rio Grande to negotiate with the authorities there. They had no success in negotiating. The colonists decided to separate from Mexico. Sterling Robertson was one of the signers of the Declaration of Independence and of the Constitution of the Republic of Texas.

When news of the fall of the Alamo reached Robertson, he packed his valuable land grants and other important papers into a strongbox. He entrusted the box to his fourteen-year-old son, Elijah, and instructed him to take the box across the Sabine River, "beyond the limits of Texas," for safekeeping. Robertson then hastened to join the army of General Sam Houston on its way to San Jacinto.

Houston's hastily assembled army defeated the Mexican General Santa Anna at San Jacinto. Gradually, the Texas settlers began to return to their homes and their land. Sterling Robertson reclaimed his valuable papers from his son, Elijah.

Volunteers had responded to Texas' call for fighting men in the battle for independence. Texas was now a Republic. The Mexican government was no longer a threat, but Indians and outlaws were.

Texas did not have a standing army. The Texas Rangers, formed by Stephen F. Austin in 1823, protected the settlers and defended the new Republic's frontiers. The Rangers were not soldiers. They were similar to a mounted militia. Their aim was to bring law and order to Texas.

For two years Robertson, then in his fifties, served as a captain with the Rangers. Elijah was a private in his father's Ranger company for four months.

In February 1841 Elijah wrote to his father, saying he had decided to go to school until he "had a license to practice law." The Texas Bar admitted him in 1845.

Texas' vast lands were the new Republic's greatest asset. Proof of land ownership often depended upon Spanish and Mexican grants. In December 1836 the First Congress established the General Land Office to assemble and translate these records. Elijah, fluent in Spanish since childhood and now a lawyer, worked for a time as a translator for the Land Office in Austin.

Elijah Robertson later moved to Bell County with his

second wife, Mary Elizabeth Dickey. There he began building his home on a high rise of land near the Salado Creek.

The first home was little more than a collection of log houses. A large white frame two-story structure with twenty-four rooms slowly replaced the cabins. Construction continued for four years, from 1856 to 1860. Wagons drawn by oxen hauled the lumber to Salado from Houston on the Texas coast. Behind the main house were servants' quarters, stables, and other buildings.

Here Elijah and Mary Elizabeth Dickey Robertson raised twelve children, six sons (including Maclin, Mary E's father) and six daughters. Robertson gave land to establish Salado College, and Mrs. Robertson organized a women's literary circle. The Robertson home became the center of Salado's social and cultural life.

History books and family records describe Elijah Robertson as "genial and courteous . . . generous to a fault." But the painting little Mary Elizabeth saw hanging in the front parlor showed a man with dark, piercing eyes, a stern expression, and a long, narrow face partly hidden by a heavy beard. Little wonder that Mary Elizabeth was too frightened to go into the room alone.

The child found the portraits of her dead ancestors intimidating. She had no such reservations about their final resting place on earth, the family cemetery. Mary Elizabeth and her numerous Robertson cousins played house among the gravestones.

As soon as her baby brother, George, could toddle, Mary Elizabeth had a special playmate. In the summers at Salado the two children invented their own games, played with the animals in the barnyard, and explored the Robertson farm. The youngsters didn't have many toys — a little red wagon sometimes, or perhaps a doll and baby buggy. They used their lively imaginations. Sticks and stones and the gnarly tree roots that spread across the top of the ground became their playthings.

At night the children gazed at the stars which filled

the clear sky over Salado. No big city lights reflected against the dark to hide the wonders of the firmament. Mary Elizabeth would recite the rhyme, "Star light, star bright, first star I see tonight . . ."

Horses, sheep, turkeys, and always a dog or two were on the Robertson farm. Mary Elizabeth helped feed the spring lambs from a milk-filled glass nursing bottle fitted with a rubber nipple. The lambs butted their heads against her legs. When she petted them, her palms felt slippery and smelled of their curly wool.

One day, when George was about three years old, his Grandmother Alice Robertson fixed him a jelly sandwich. He bounced out the back door, holding the sandwich in both hands. Just as he raised the bread to his mouth to take a bite, a big turkey swooped at him. Flapping its outspread wings furiously, the turkey snatched the sandwich away.

George couldn't believe what had just happened to him. But there was the turkey, dashing across the yard, head held high, red wattle waggling, with the thick chunk of bread clinched in its beak.

George ran back into the house. "That gobbler stole my jelly bread!" he cried.

Grandmother Alice hid her smile as she registered her grandson's indignation. "I'll make you another one. Perhaps you'd like to eat this one here at the kitchen table," she suggested tactfully.

Grandmother Alice usually kept one or two dogs around the place for company and protection. A large black-and-tan Airedale terrier named Tessie and a mixed-breed, part bloodhound called Red were fiercely protective. Grandmother ordered her groceries by telephone from Norwood's store in Salado. Norwood would deliver the groceries, but only after Grandmother Alice penned the watchdogs.

Late one summer evening the women and children were alone in the large house. The men were away on business. Mary E was reading aloud, as she often did.

Mary Elizabeth and the other children gathered around her.

Outside, Tessie and Red suddenly started a terrible racket. They never barked that way at any of the family.

Mary E left the room for a moment, then came back, seated herself, and resumed reading. George's eyes widened, but he didn't say anything. In the folds of his mother's full skirt he had glimpsed her pistol.

Mary E hadn't forgotten how to shoot, but there was no skunk in the hen house that night. Whatever — or whoever — had spooked the dogs passed on by.

Their mother never tired of reading aloud to the children. She was eager to share with them the literature that meant so much to her own life. The Bible and the works of Shakespeare were so familiar to her she could supply a suitable quotation for any situation. The lilt and rhythm of the beloved British poets entered the family's language.

The library in the Salado home was one of Mary Elizabeth's favorite rooms. She ran her fingers over the fine bindings and inhaled the leathery smell of the books. She promised herself that someday she would read them all.

In the late afternoons, with George running to keep up with her, Mary Elizabeth often crossed the pasture. She stood on the rise of land at the edge of the Robertson property. From there she could look over the fence and gaze down at the road and the growing numbers of passing automobiles.

Where does the road go? she wondered. *Where will it take me?*

She was soon to learn the answers, with frightening and painful consequences.

4. The Road Traveled

One day a frisky yellow puppy showed up at the Robertson farm in Salado. Tommy fed him, as he did most of the strays that came around. One more dog made little difference. Grandmother Alice always kept dogs on the Robertson place.

The puppy grew plump on table scraps. It was quite happy to waddle along behind Tommy wherever he went.

Tommy left for the summer to work with his father on road construction. The puppy attached his devotion to the other children. Mary Elizabeth was almost five years old. George was not yet three.

Gradually, the children began to notice changes in the yellow puppy's behavior. He lost interest in his favorite activity — eating. He seemed to have trouble swallowing. He no longer enjoyed chasing after the children and joining in their games. He just wanted to snooze. He became irritable when the children tried to wake him.

"He probably misses Tommy," Mary Elizabeth decided.

George was playing near the front gate one day. For no reason the yellow puppy began nipping at him. George tried to push the animal away, but it only grew more determined. Sinking its needle-sharp teeth into George's leg, it bit hard.

The bite hurt. Frightened and in pain, George began to cry.

Mary Elizabeth came running when she heard her baby brother cry. She tugged the puppy off George, then held the squirming animal tightly in her arms. It turned its anger on her, biting her hand. George ran to the house.

Usually calm and serene, Mary E was alarmed when the children told her what had happened. Even more so when her twelve-year-old daughter Alice reluctantly admitted the yellow dog also had bitten her.

"It's nothing," Alice insisted. "Just a scratch."

Mary E favored cats rather than dogs. Still, she'd been around dogs all her life. She knew this puppy's behavior was not normal.

"Dear Lord," she prayed softly, "don't let that puppy be mad."

A mad dog — one with rabies, or hydrophobia as people often called the disease — was a terrifying possibility. Rabies was not uncommon in the Texas heat.

Mary E cleaned the wounds carefully. She knew that wasn't any protection. If the puppy were rabid, its saliva had transferred the rabies virus to the youngsters when it bit them. Left untreated, the disease was fatal. The treatment was difficult to obtain, long, and painful.

There was only one way to be certain. They must send the puppy's head to the laboratory in Austin. Mary E's brothers, Sterling and Maclin, took care of that sad but necessary task. Doctors in the laboratory would examine the animal's brain under a microscope.

Meanwhile Mary E watched over her three children anxiously. Did they have headaches? Fever? Trouble swallowing?

At last the test results came back from Austin. There was no mistake. The puppy had been rabid.

Time was crucial now. The children had to begin receiving treatments at once.

Mary E packed their clothes and a few personal belongings they would need. Her brothers drove her and her three children to Austin.

At last Mary Elizabeth discovered where the road past the Salado house led. The child watched eagerly and soaked up every detail. She asked her mother and uncles hundreds of questions.

Mary E took a room at the Rutledge Boarding House, 4005 Guadalupe Street in Austin. Many of the boarders were there for the same purpose. They were in Austin to receive treatment for rabies at the Pasteur Institute. The institute was across the street on the grounds of the State Hospital.

Every morning the family walked across Guadalupe Street to the treatment center. The children received painful injections of vaccine serum into the soft abdominal muscles.

Alice still couldn't believe her tiny scratch warranted such extreme measures. George couldn't understand why people wanted to hurt him. Mary Elizabeth was simply impatient to be done with the shots and get on with more important things. She looked forward to their daily treat of ice cream.

Austin was the capital of Texas, but in 1925 it was not a large city. Still, it was larger than Belton. Mary Elizabeth wanted to go everywhere and see everything. She loved sightseeing.

The summer heat was scorching. One day the temperature reached 104 degrees. In the evening, if the day cooled off enough, the family took walks in the Hyde Park neighborhood.

Mary Elizabeth's mother had never learned to drive and didn't have an automobile. Money was scarce. There was barely enough to pay for the expensive Pasteur treatments and room and board at the Rutledges'. Even so, Mary E kept her children occupied. She couldn't pass up the opportunity to add to their knowledge. She didn't want them to have time to dread the next day's treatment.

When she had a moment to herself, Mary E eagerly read the *Austin Statesman* and the *Austin American.* Like all of her family, she had a keen interest in politics. Women's right to vote had been recognized in August 1920. Now, a scant five years later, a woman governor lived in the Governor's Mansion.

The woman, Miriam A. Wallace Ferguson, was a native of Bell County. She and her husband, James E. Ferguson, grew up near Salado. The Fergusons may have been "home folks," but the Robertsons and Sutherlands didn't agree with their politics. Mary E had no patience with the Fergusons' lack of financial support for the University of Texas.

Jim Ferguson had been elected governor in 1914. He served a two-year term and was reelected in 1916. Shortly into his second term, Ferguson was impeached and convicted on various charges, including misuse of state funds. He was barred from holding any elected state office.

Miriam, or "Ma," Ferguson announced her candidacy in 1924. Few voters doubted it was her husband's way of getting back into power. One of the Ferguson campaign slogans was "Two governors for the price of one!"

Of course, anything the first woman governor did was news — from her homemade peach preserves and biscuits to the "simple black-and-white frock" she wore to an official function.

Mrs. Ferguson, only a few months into her first term of office, already was drawing criticism for some of her policies — her husband's policies, some people said.

Mary E noticed another item in the newspaper, one of even greater personal interest to her. According to the article, the cost for a boy or girl to attend the University of Texas for one year was a staggering $348.

Mary E caught her breath as she reread the story. That amount, the writer assured her, was moderate.

Without careful budgeting, the total could easily run to almost twice that amount.

Tommy, the oldest son, would soon graduate from Belton High School. Alice was not far behind. Mary E was determined to give each of her children the best education possible. How on earth could they manage those costs?

As she read the article for a third time, she saw that room and board and heating fuel accounted for the larger share of the expenses. She began to have a plan.

By the following summer, Mary Elizabeth had managed to forget the painful treatments at the Pasteur Institute in Austin. She was delighted to be back in Salado for the summer of 1926. When the summer ended she would celebrate her sixth birthday. How she anticipated the event! At last she'd be old enough to go to school.

One day early in June, horses and wagons and almost as many automobiles choked Salado's main street. A crowd gathered in front of the empty First State Bank building. The bank had been closed since 1920. Mary Elizabeth was used to seeing the deserted building. What could draw so many people? Why were they laughing and cheering?

Curious, she edged her way through the excited throng. Even before she could see the cause of all the commotion, she heard a man's voice thundering out over the crowd.

"Poor?" he asked. "Why, we were poor as Job's turkey!"

The man was Jim Ferguson. He was describing his childhood on a farm near Salado.

Mary Elizabeth was accustomed to hearing her family discuss politics and government, sometimes late into the night. These talks might range from humorous to earnest. But Mary Elizabeth had never heard a speaker like this one. It was the first political campaign speech she had ever heard.

Jim Ferguson was still very popular with rural Texans. They believed he understood the problems of the farmers and the people who lived in small country towns.

Now, in the summer of 1926, "Farmer Jim," as folks called him, was stumping the state, campaigning for his wife's election to a second term.

Mary Elizabeth looked up at the tall speaker. To her young eyes he appeared to be an old man. He was nearly fifty-five, but the people who had come to hear him could still see signs of the husky, hard-working youth he had been. He loved to talk to a crowd, and the crowd loved to listen. When he paused for breath or effect, his attentive audience cheered him with shouts of "Give it to 'em, Jim!"

Jim grew warm from the heat of the day and his impassioned oration. He yanked off his coat, peeled off his vest, unknotted his tie, and wiped the sweat from his brow with a big handkerchief.

"I'm not gonna throw mud in this campaign," he promised the crowd. "I'm gonna throw *rocks*!" He leaned back, hooking his thumbs under his colorful galluses.

His listeners thundered their approval. Farmer Jim was one of them — one of the common man.

Mary Elizabeth was as excited as anyone in the crowd. The enthusiasm was contagious. She was too young to understand the issues, but she thought the idea of having a woman governor was perfectly natural.

Before Mary Elizabeth could settle into her summer in Salado, Mother had a surprise. "We're going to Cleburne to be with your father this summer," Mary E told her children. "He's building roads there. Tommy's going to help him."

Mary E and her older daughter, Alice, packed the clothes and household goods the family would need. With Mary Elizabeth, George, and the children's young aunt, Frances Lucille Sutherland, they all piled into an open Model T Ford for the hundred-mile trip to Cleburne.

Family members expressed shock when they heard that Tommy would drive.

"Mary E, surely you're not going to let a fourteen-year-old boy drive an automobile!" they said.

"He knows how to drive," Mary E replied calmly. "I

don't. He's a very good driver. His father taught him. He's had lots of practice driving in the pasture and on the country roads."

In 1926, Texas law had no provision for licensing drivers of any age. People believed that if a boy could ride a horse or drive a horse-drawn wagon, he could drive an automobile.

Cleburne was almost three times the size of Belton. Transportation had played a big role in the town's growth. Like Salado, Cleburne began as a stagecoach stop. Since 1911 an electric railway system, called the Interurban, linked Cleburne with nearby Fort Worth. The depots, shops, and roundhouses of the Santa Fe Railroad employed many of the town's workers.

Now, in the summer of 1926, Cleburne and Johnson County wanted roads — good, hard-surfaced roads for automobiles, trucks, and buses.

Mary Elizabeth's father rented a comfortable white frame house for the summer so his family could be near him as he helped to build the roads.

While Tom and Tommy worked on the roads, Mary E, Alice, and Lucille tended to household chores. They had many meals to prepare. Plump fruits and fresh vegetables from Johnson County's many truck farms were abundant. Mary Elizabeth and George were free to play on the big porch or under the shade of a tall sycamore tree in the yard. One day Mary Elizabeth burst into the kitchen. She claimed a big wooden spoon and an old saucepan for some game she and George had devised. She hurled her small self out the door and back to play.

Mary E shook her head in wry amusement. *My kingdom and stars!* she thought. *Looking at that child is like looking in a mirror at myself when I was five years old. But she has her father's personality and energy. Never still for a moment.*

The summer would have been nearly perfect for Mary Elizabeth except for grasshoppers. Swarms of them infested Cleburne in July 1926.

"They're in my hair and in my mouth and on my dress," she complained to Tommy.

Mary Elizabeth loved to ride in the automobile, but even that provided no relief from the pests. The Model T Ford was open, so there was no way to keep the leaping insects out.

"You can't go *anywhere* without grasshoppers," she declared.

At the end of the summer the family decided to send Mary Elizabeth, Tommy, and their young Aunt Lucille back by train. On the morning of the first day of September, the children went to the Santa Fe depot. Tommy and Lucille bought their tickets. They waited impatiently until the train roared in.

Up ahead Mary Elizabeth could see the orange-red glow of fire in the puffing steam locomotive. As they boarded the train, Tommy gave her a boost and the conductor leaned down to help her. The steps to the coach car were higher than her legs were long.

She clambered up on the seat and ran her fingers over the varnished wood and gleaming brass fittings. In her lap she held the cardboard box of lunch that Mary E had prepared for her.

The whistle blew and the train rolled out of the station. The motion of the wheels revolving rhythmically beneath her rocked Mary Elizabeth gently from side to side.

"Now *this,*" she sighed contentedly, "is the way to travel."

Tommy regarded his small sister with fond humor. "You like this train better than the Tin Lizzie?" he teased.

"Well, of course!" Mary Elizabeth replied. "The grasshoppers can't get on the train."

The train had scarcely chugged up to a good speed before the conductor started making his way along the aisle, saying, "Tickets. Tickets, please." He punched the tickets offered by the passengers and visited for a moment with each.

Tommy and his Aunt Lucille presented their tickets.

"We've been in Cleburne all summer," Tommy told the smiling conductor. "Now we're going home to Belton."

"And besides that," Mary Elizabeth piped up, "today is my birthday. I'm six years old today."

The conductor's smile vanished. He looked troubled. "Well, in that case," he said reluctantly, "I'm afraid I'll have to ask you for a ticket."

Tommy recognized the problem immediately. Children under the age of six could ride the train free. No one had remembered that Mary Elizabeth would need a ticket today.

"It's all right, Conductor," Tommy spoke up quickly. "She wasn't born till evening, so she's still only five years old."

The conductor winked at Tommy and continued down the aisle.

5. Belton School Bells

Mary Elizabeth studied her teacher as Miss Nellie Duckworth looked over her classroom of brand new first-graders. Miss Duckworth was young and pretty. Her smile, Mary Elizabeth decided, was as sweet as Mary E's.

"Children, you may open your books."

Mary Elizabeth wriggled closer to her wooden school desk.

Open your books. Miss Duckworth might just as well have said, *Open your world.* To Mary Elizabeth the meaning was the same. Now she'd be able to read all those books in the Robertson library, just as she had promised herself.

She had looked forward to this day. She knew how highly her family valued education. And now she was six years old, in the first grade of Tyler Ward School in Belton, ready to learn everything. Like the other girls, Mary Elizabeth wore a cotton dress, long cotton stockings, and a sweater.

"I love my teacher," she declared as she burst into the Sutherland home that afternoon. "School is fun."

Mary Elizabeth hurled herself into school with the same energy and enthusiasm she brought to all her projects. She had a keen eye for details and delighted in reporting them to her family.

Tommy's first day was not quite so pleasant. A good-looking youngster, he was tall for his age. Four Belton boys challenged the newcomer. Tommy was never sure who won the fight, but they all became close friends.

For the next several days Tommy and Alice listened with varying degrees of patience as Mary Elizabeth described her classroom. The children kept their coats in a cloakroom. A big picture of George Washington hung above the blackboard behind Miss Duckworth's desk. Cardboard strips showing how to write numbers and letters of the alphabet ran across the top of the blackboard.

The desks and seats had wrought-iron legs, bolted to the floor. Each child's small wooden desk had an inkwell — a round cutout to hold a bottle of ink. The children dipped the nibs of their writing pens into the ink. Sometimes mischievous boys tried to dip girls' pigtails into the ink instead.

Mary Elizabeth delighted in the nose-tickling smells: the empty cigar box to hold her pencils, the chalk, the waxy crayons, the heavy construction paper and gooey white paste, the sawdust used to sweep the wooden floors.

But a few things about school puzzled Mary Elizabeth.

All her young life she had played almost daily with her numerous Sutherland and Robertson kin, both boys and girls. Now, at school, her teachers told her she must play only with the other girls, on the girls' side of the playground. They played tag, jump rope, and jacks. Sometimes they played Kick the Can and Red Rover, Red Rover. Boys played on their own side of the playground. They played rough-and-tumble team games.

Mary Elizabeth's older sister, Alice, liked going to school in Belton too. Classes in Salado had grown small, but Tyler Ward was a big school, with many other youngsters her own age.

Alice eagerly filled out her enrollment papers. In the blank for "Father's occupation" she wrote: *Highwayman.*

"Your daddy builds highways, dear," Mary E told her daughter gently. "That's not quite the same thing as a highwayman."

Alice came home from school one day and said, "Miss Birdwell asked us today to name our favorite household chores."

Mary Elizabeth's hazel eyes grew large. My kingdom, but they asked hard questions in the fifth grade! Think as she might, Mary Elizabeth couldn't imagine liking *any* household task, let alone having a favorite.

"And what did you tell your teacher?" Mary E smiled at her older daughter. Alice had always been a great help around the house, joining in willingly with her mother and aunts.

"Oh, that's easy. I like washing dishes best," Alice answered.

"Why's that?"

"Because," Alice explained, "I play like each dish is one of my little babies, and I'm giving each of them a bath."

Two Belton women called on Mary E one day. She was in the midst of boiling and scrubbing the family's laundry, but she greeted her visitors graciously.

"We came by to invite you to join our ladies' club," one of them said.

Mary E managed a weary smile. "I'm sorry," she said. "My children are my club. They're all I have time for."

Crime became a serious problem in the 1920s. Not just in New York and Chicago, but in Texas and even in Belton. Many people blamed Prohibition, which outlawed the legal sale of alcohol. Hard economic times, unemployment, and the changes in people's way of living as they moved from the country to towns and cities also played a part.

With Tom Sutherland away from home, building highways, Mary E was often alone with her children. One day a cousin, coming to play with Tommy, was surprised to find the front door open. He walked into the house and found Mary E sitting in the living room, reading.

"Aunt Mary E," he asked, "why don't you keep your door locked? Aren't you afraid someone bad might just walk in?"

Mary E lifted a corner of the *Saturday Evening Post* in her lap. There was her Colt revolver, the long ago gift from her father, Maclin Robertson.

After school Tommy and two of his closest friends, Thomas Gordon Saunders and Barney Buck Taylor, made the rounds. First they went to Tommy's house, then the others'. At each they pretended starvation and begged for milk and cookies or tea cakes.

Sometimes their pranks were not so innocent.

They climbed onto the bridge that crossed over the Belton-Temple Interurban trolley tracks. Overhead electric cables powered the trolley. The boys discovered that if they all grabbed hold of the guy wire and shook it hard enough, they could disconnect the wire from the power rod to the electric trolley below.

"We cut off power to the trolley," Tommy bragged to his family one evening. "We stopped that trolley dead! You should have seen all those people scrambling around down there trying to figure out what to do."

"I was *on* that trolley," Tom Sutherland roared. "You rascal, I'll skin you alive!"

Only the pleading of his young Aunt Florence saved Tommy from a whipping. Next day Tommy met the equally repentant Barney Buck and Thomas Gordon. Apparently none of the grownups had appreciated the humor of the incident.

In spite of his playful disposition, Tommy was an excellent student. He made good grades in English literature. That was not surprising to Mary E. She had shared her love of the British poets with him when he was just a toddler on the Raney Ranch in South Texas.

Now, at Belton High School, Tommy was editor of his school's annual magazine, *Tiger Tales*. Miss Virginia

Smith, Tommy's English teacher, was young and attractive. Every male student in her class had a romantic crush on her.

Tommy was also doing very well in Spanish. He had learned to speak Spanish fluently, first from his father and later from the Mexican laborers with whom he worked on road crews. His Spanish teacher, Alton Parker Thomason, was impressed with Tommy's natural ability plus his willingness to study and learn. He urged Tommy to go to the University of Texas.

Even as Mary E listened to her children's excited recitals of their daily activities, her mind always drifted back to her problem. How could she manage to send her oldest son, Tommy, to the University of Texas?

Tommy's young aunt, Mabel, had graduated from Belton High School with top honors. She had gone to Houston to study comtometry. Tommy would graduate at the end of the year.

Then Mary E remembered reading in the newspaper that room and board accounted for most of the cost of attending the University of Texas. *Well,* Mary E thought to herself, *I'll just move the whole family to Austin. That way, the children can live at home and go to the university.*

Tommy graduated with honors. He was salutatorian of his high school class. As an Eagle Scout in the Heart of Texas Council, he received a small scholarship toward his university tuition.

With the help of her husband and brothers, Mary E loaded up the family and moved to Austin.

6. The Great Depression

Mary E rented a big, Victorian-style house at 110 East Twenty-second Street. The house was close to the university and to Mary Elizabeth's school. The children could walk to school.

In September, Mary Elizabeth entered the second grade at Wooldridge Elementary School on West Twenty-fourth Street. The school building itself was forty years old and rather crowded. Children of university professors attended Wooldridge. Everyone said it was the best elementary school in Austin.

On her first day at school Mary Elizabeth met another new student, Sue Kone. Her family had just moved to Austin from Yuma, Arizona. The two young girls quickly became best friends.

Mary Elizabeth's family had always been interested in politics. She had grown up listening to their discussions. The tone changed, however, in the summer of 1928.

"Mary E, you can't be thinking of voting for a *Republican*!" Mary Elizabeth heard her father say.

Texas was a one-party state, and that party was

Democratic. Within the party, however, voters often split on issues and personalities. In 1928 Texans and many other Democrats were seriously divided on the national candidates.

The Eighteenth Amendment to the Constitution, enforced by the Volstead Act, prohibited the sale of liquor. Prohibition was a popular idea at the close of World War I. Now, a decade later, voters were sharply divided. Many blamed bootlegging for the rise in crime throughout the country.

Alfred E. Smith, former governor of New York, was the Democratic party's nominee for president. He was Roman Catholic. He supported the "wet" side; that is, he opposed Prohibition.

Democrats, for the most part, were rural Protestants. Even staunchly loyal Democrats were reluctant to vote for a man they associated with corrupt big city politics and Catholicism.

Mary E's values were firmly rooted in rural Salado and the Methodist Church. She was unwilling to vote for Al Smith just because he was the Democratic candidate.

The Republican party, at its national convention in Kansas City, nominated Herbert Hoover on June 15, 1928. Hoover was a mid-Westerner, a Quaker, and "dry." He supported Prohibition. Hoover campaigned on the promise of a return to prosperity. His slogan was, "A car in every garage and a chicken in every pot."

As many as ten percent of American workers were without jobs. Mary Elizabeth's father now was one of them. Nevertheless, he intended to vote a straight Democratic ticket.

Mary Elizabeth's mother was a soft-spoken, gentle woman with a mind of her own.

"We women earned the right to vote in 1920," she reminded her husband firmly. "I'll make my own choice."

Whatever Mary E's choice may have been, large numbers of Texas Democrats, calling themselves "Hoovercrats," voted for the Republican candidate. Hoover won the election, November 6, 1928. He was sworn into office Monday, March 4, 1929, as the thirty-first president.

Times were hard for the Sutherland family. Mary E bought the family's groceries at the Wukasch Fancy Groceries and Fruits, 2000 Guadalupe Street. Few of Joe A. Wukasch's customers had cash to pay for their food. He put the groceries on their bill in an account book.

Tommy got a job in the university cafeteria to help with expenses. Finding that the work interfered with his studying, he soon decided to concentrate on his classes.

One morning, when Mary Elizabeth was in the third grade, she woke up feeling rotten. Instead of bouncing out of bed as usual, she called hoarsely to her mother.

"I don't feel good," she said. "My throat hurts."

Mary E came quickly. She saw that her daughter's face was flushed. Her forehead felt hot to the touch. Her throat was an angry red.

Mary E called a doctor. He confirmed her fears: Mary Elizabeth had scarlet fever.

The house was quarantined. A person from the health department came out and tacked a big red cardboard sign on the front door.

Quarantine was a method used to help prevent the spread of infectious diseases. For the period of quarantine, the occupants of the house had to remain inside, and no one else was permitted to come in.

On the second day, Mary Elizabeth broke out in the bright scarlet rash that gave the disease its name.

Mary E nursed her daughter. She tempted her appetite with homemade soup. She spent hours reading to her. She boiled and scalded dishes and linens from the sick room to protect the rest of the family.

Sue Kone came by to walk to school with Mary Elizabeth and was surprised to see the quarantine sign. Someone in the family was sick. Was it her friend Mary Elizabeth? Sue stood outside on the sidewalk, reluctant to leave.

Mary E saw the small child standing in front of the house. She opened the front door and called out to her.

"Mary Elizabeth is sick, but she'll be just fine," Mary E assured her daughter's friend.

Tommy submitted unwillingly to the quarantine for a day or so. Then he began slipping out of the house to attend his classes. Soon he was sneaking friends into the house for study sessions.

By the sixth day the fever and the rash were gone. So were handfuls of Mary Elizabeth's thick, chestnut brown hair. Her skin was peeling and she itched all over. She was feeling too weak to be up but much too well to stay in bed. She wanted to *do something!*

"Why don't you write a song for your school?" Mary E suggested, bringing her pencil and paper.

To the tune of "Maryland," Mary Elizabeth composed the words: "Wooldridge School, my Wooldridge School."

Sue Kone came by every day after school to check on her friend's recovery. She would stand on the sidewalk in front of the house and wait for Mary E to notice her and call out a report.

One day the red cardboard sign was gone. Sue knew what that must mean: Mary Elizabeth was dead!

Sue dropped her books. She sat down on the curb and began to cry.

Mary E rushed out to the sobbing child.

"Is Mary Elizabeth dead?" Sue asked fearfully.

"Oh, no, Sue," Mary E assured her. "She's well now. That's why they've taken down the quarantine sign. Mary Elizabeth will be back in school Monday."

Despite promises that good times were "just around the corner," times grew harder for the Sutherlands. Jobs were scarce and competition for them was fierce. Tom Sutherland took any job he could get.

The whole country suffered. People blamed the president. His name became associated with the signs of the Depression. In Austin and the rest of the country, camps where the homeless gathered sprang up under bridges and near railroad tracks. The camps were called

"Hoovervilles." People slept under newspapers they called "Hoover blankets."

Hoboes, as the jobless, drifting men were called, often came to the door to ask for food. In exchange they worked around the house or yard. Although the Sutherlands seldom had enough food for themselves, Mary Elizabeth never saw her mother turn anyone away hungry.

In the spring Mary E knew she was pregnant again. This delivery would be the most difficult of all. This time, however, she was in a hospital, attended by a doctor. She received ether, an anesthetic to ease the pain. Her fifth child, a son, William Gordon Sutherland, was born October 12, 1929. He weighed a scant three pounds. The strain of prolonged labor left Mary E without her eyesight for a period of time.

Grandmother Robertson came to Austin from Salado to help care for the tiny infant. Billy was so small she was afraid he would smother in his blankets. She hovered over him, listening for the sound of his breathing. Fifteen-year-old Alice, who always loved children, looked after Mary Elizabeth and George.

On October 29, "Black Tuesday," the New York stock market crashed. The great promise of prosperity had failed. The Great Depression had begun.

Nine-year-old Mary Elizabeth stood in the hall, staring at her father through the open door of the bathroom. The day was February 22, 1930. Tom Sutherland was on his knees beside the big claw-footed bathtub. He whistled as he energetically scrubbed a tubful of laundry.

"Here it is, Washington's birthday," he said jovially when he noticed his small daughter watching him. "And I'm washing Billy's diapers! Washing diapers on Washington's birthday. Washing diapers on Washington's birthday." He turned the words into a cheerful song.

Mary E was recovering very slowly from Billy's birth. Tom was unable to find steady work during the Depression. Whenever he was home he willingly turned his hand to any task that needed doing. Everyone in the house pitched in to help.

Robertson cousins and other university students began staying with the Sutherlands. Mary E soon had so many people crowded into the house she needed a larger place. The family moved and then moved again.

They finally settled into a large, three-story house at 1611 West Avenue. The family always called the home simply by the address, 1611.

Grandmother Robertson suffered a stroke. She wasn't able to help around the house much, but she did what she could.

Malcolm McLean, a cousin from Belton, stayed with the Sutherland family at 1611 while he attended the university. He slept on a cot on the screened porch. One day he discovered someone had neatly darned the holes in his socks.

"Aunt Mary E, who darned my socks?" he asked.

Mary E smiled and nodded toward Grandmother Robertson.

In such a large family, with so many cousins of nearly the same age, there was never a shortage of good, clean, everyday clothes. The family never discarded a garment if it could be passed on. Mary Elizabeth and Alice especially looked forward to boxes from their Aunt Alice, Mary E's sister. Aunt Alice had married James Marion West, Jr., the son of "Silver Dollar" Jim West, a wealthy Houston businessman. Aunt Alice did much to help her family through the hard times. Getting a box of clothes from Aunt Alice was always an exciting event. The clothes were newer and more stylish. The only problem was that Aunt Alice often forgot to pack the matching belts or other accessories.

Mary Elizabeth and her sister, Alice, would dig eagerly into the big box. They would hold the dresses up to themselves, giggling as they selected or exchanged one or another.

"I want this one," Mary Elizabeth would say, claiming a blue cotton dress with puffed sleeves and a white collar. "If I can find the belt!"

Food was another matter. The people in the house at 1611 never went hungry, but mealtimes didn't offer much variety. Mary E abandoned the pot of beans simmering on the back of the stove. She favored a new product: canned pork and beans. She added rice and cornbread to the meal, with occasional meatloaf when she could afford it. Banana pudding was the favorite dessert.

Sometimes on pleasant Sunday afternoons the family went out in the country south of town to visit the Faulk family. Judge Henry Faulk and his wife, Martha (Miss Mattie), had a big, comfortable house tumbling with children. There were two sons, John Henry, Jr., and Hamilton, and three daughters, Mary, Martha, and Texana. The families sat on the shady porch, drinking cool buttermilk and enjoying the fine art of good conversation.

At home Mary E was mother, hostess, counselor, tutor, and scholar-in-residence for the people in 1611. With her fine white hair piled high, her brown eyes sparkling, and her serene nature evident, she presided over the table.

The evening meal was a time for everyone to gather at the big round table and share the events of their day. They chattered eagerly about school activities, a good book they had read, the newspaper headlines, a funny radio program, the newest big band recording, the latest dance craze, perhaps a movie or a play they had seen. And always, politics.

7. 1611 West Avenue

When the presidential elections rolled around again, the voters were not as divided as they had been in 1928. The country blamed the Republican president, Herbert Hoover, for the Depression.

Franklin D. Roosevelt, a Democrat, promised a "New Deal." He won the election on November 8, 1932, with an overwhelming plurality.

Mary Elizabeth and her family gathered around the radio on March 4, 1933, Inauguration Day. They listened as the new president took the oath of office in Washington, D.C. and then addressed the nation. In a clear, strong voice, he said, "The only thing we have to fear is fear itself!"

After the address, the U.S. Cavalry bugle corps played "Ruffles and Flourishes."

Mary Elizabeth felt a shiver of excitement. Politics was just about the most exciting thing she could imagine. Just picture being in Washington!

A Texan, John Nance Garner from Uvalde, was the new vice president. Mary E used the opportunity to tell

Mary Elizabeth about other Texans in national politics. She pointed out the red brick house across the street from 1611.

"It's a university fraternity house now," she explained, "but originally it was the home of Edward Mandell House and his wife, Loulie." Colonel House was a close friend and adviser to President Woodrow Wilson during World War I. Mary E admired President Wilson. She often talked to the children about him.

Mary E also loved to retell stories about her aunts, Louella and Birdie, and their husbands. Louella Robertson was a daughter of E. Sterling C. Robertson and Mary Elizabeth Dickey. Louella made a passionate plea for equal educational opportunities for women. Her zeal attracted the attention of a handsome young lawyer, Zachary Taylor Fulmore. They married at Salado in 1877 and moved to Austin.

"Mr. Fulmore's law partner was Mr. A. P. Wooldridge," Mary E told her daughter, using the formal style of her generation. "Yes, the same Mr. Wooldridge for whom your school is named. Mr. Fulmore became attorney to Colonel House.

"My Aunt Birdie — Eliza Sophia Robertson — married Mr. Cone Johnson," Mary E continued.

Cone Johnson was a lawyer from Tyler. He became active in the Democratic party, and so did Birdie. Like her older sister Louella, Birdie believed in education for women. Legislators of the time didn't believe women needed education. A college education, some argued, might even interfere with what they thought was a woman's function in life — bearing children. Birdie worked with other women, Helen Stoddard and Eleanor Brackenridge of San Antonio. Finally, the women succeeded.

An act of the Texas legislature in 1901 created the Girls Industrial College at Denton. Birdie Johnson served eleven years on the college's Board of Regents. The name was later changed to College of Industrial Arts, Texas State College for Women, and finally, in 1957, Texas Woman's University.

Birdie Johnson was also a suffragist. Suffrage leaders believed women had a right to vote. After all, political decisions affected the lives of women as well as men. Birdie attended Democratic conventions with her husband and eagerly took part in politics.

In 1914 President Wilson appointed Cone Johnson solicitor in the Department of State. The Johnsons lived in Washington until 1917.

"I wish I'd been alive in those days," Mary Elizabeth said wistfully. "I'd love to have been in Washington. That's where everything happens!"

Some things happened in Texas, of course. Texas politics never lacked excitement or colorful personalities.

The evening supper conversations at 1611 usually centered around the day's political issue. In 1933 Miriam Ferguson was serving her second term as governor.

Mary Elizabeth's family strongly opposed the Fergusons because of their stand on financing for the University of Texas. Mrs. Ferguson had never been a strong supporter of women's suffrage. However, some women suffragists worked on her behalf in her first campaign. Many, including Jane Yelvington McCallum and Minnie Fisher Cunningham, later threw their efforts into the campaign of Dan Moody. "Dan's the Man" became the popular slogan.

Moody was a young lawyer from Georgetown in Williamson County. He had been attorney general during Mrs. Ferguson's first term. When he had become governor in January 1927, he named Mrs. McCallum as his secretary of state.

On her thirteenth birthday, September 1, 1933, Mary Elizabeth received a letter from her brother, Tommy:

> Dear Mary Elizabeth,
>
> Congratulations on having gotten into your teens . . . Really there's more to your teens (that you remember) than to all the rest of your life put together . . .

Tommy had graduated from the university in 1931 and was working on his master's degree when he and Lois Peyton Hartley met. He planned to marry his "Charleston belle" on November 25, 1933.

Tom Sutherland rushed in from his work in West Texas for the ceremony. He was dressed more like the rancher he had been than the road contractor he had become. He enjoyed wearing Western shirts and Stetson hats.

The Depression made money scarce. The young couple decided on a simple evening ceremony at 1611. They didn't have the usual attendants. Billy, just turned four, and his five-year-old cousin, Lauranne Sutherland, made an aisle of satin ribbons for the couple.

Tommy had borrowed money to buy the wedding ring. When he stumbled over a line in the vows, his cousin Malcolm McLean whispered, "With this ring, I'm in the red."

Tom Sutherland gave his son and new daughter-in-law a Chevrolet as a wedding present.

Most mornings Mary Elizabeth hurriedly finished her favorite breakfast of hot cocoa and cinnamon toast. She wanted time to read the Austin newspaper before anyone else did.

"I see you've already read this morning's newspaper," Malcolm said one day.

Mary Elizabeth looked up in innocent surprise. "How can you tell?"

Malcolm silently pointed to the buttery cinnamon fingerprints and dried cocoa splashes on the front page.

Mary Elizabeth soon was publishing her own newspaper. With her chums Sue Kone and Eugenia Worley, she went to the University Methodist Church every Saturday afternoon. Their Sunday school teacher was Mrs. Lena Hickman. The girls cranked out pages of Sunday school news on the church's mimeograph machine.

"We get as much of this purple mimeograph stuff on our fingers as we do on the paper," Eugenia pointed out.

Most evenings Alice and George washed the supper

dishes and straightened the kitchen. Before Tommy married, he had helped with the work. And he had entertained them, telling stories or reciting poems he had written. The children missed him.

Eventually, one of them would pretend to notice Mary Elizabeth's absence.

"Where's Mary Elizabeth?"

They sang out the answer: "She's on the phone with Miss Sue Kone!"

With a glance of mild irritation over her shoulder, Mary Elizabeth continued her eager, whispered conversation. The two close friends were always plotting something.

One of their favorite activities revolved around author Carolyn Keene's fictional heroine, Nancy Drew. Liz, Sue Kone, Eugenia Worley, and Nona Frances Rundell read and swapped the latest copies of *The Secret of the Old Clock, Sign of the Twisted Candle,* and *Password of Larkspur Lane.* They formed a club, the Mystery Seekers Clan, and met at a different girl's home each week.

The club members sleuthed around the neighborhood searching for secret letters, hidden wills, haunted houses, and ghostly appearances. They didn't have a little blue roadster like Nancy's, but they did have a Model T Ford they called Petunia Bell. The car belonged to all of the girls but it stayed at 1611. Some afternoons they all piled into Petunia Bell and went to Lamme's Candies on Congress Avenue for "Gems," a delicious frozen confection. Sometimes they went to Eldridge Moore's Drug Store for a Coke.

The girls ventured out of town one day. The car sank into the sandy shoulder of an unpaved road. This time there were no laughing King Ranch *vaqueros* to haul the car out. The girls were so dirty by the time they got the car back on the road, they decided to wash off in a nearby creek.

They took off their clothes and plunged into the cool water. They were splashing merrily when Patti Nolen sounded the alarm. "Look out! Someone's coming!"

A man drove his pickup truck onto the low-water bridge. With a bucket and cloth, he began to wash his truck.

There was no way the girls could get back to their clothes on the bank without being seen. So, they crouched in water up to their necks, unobserved, until the man finally drove off.

One evening, as George and Alice were washing the supper dishes, someone cried out: "Fire! Fire! The attic's on fire!"

George snatched the silver out of the pan of rinse water, grabbed the pan, and raced up the stairs to the attic. He half expected the alarm to be someone's idea of a joke.

As he reached the third floor he detected the choking billows of smoke even before he saw the red-orange flames eating away at the wallboard. He splashed the tub of water on the fire and rushed downstairs for more.

A law student living in the attic gathered up his costly law books, knotted them in a blanket, and leaned out the window.

Alice had run out of the house at the cry of fire. She was standing below, looking up.

"Here!" the student yelled down at her. "Catch these."

Alice obediently stretched out her arms. But she had underestimated the full impact of a legal education. The bundle of books sent her sprawling, knocking the breath from her.

Before George could draw another pan of water and run back upstairs, firemen from the nearby station arrived. They quickly put out the small fire. There was very little damage. The family never figured out what caused the fire.

In June 1935, flood waters rampaged along the Colorado River through Austin. The flood weakened the Austin Dam, filled homes near Barton Springs, and damaged or destroyed businesses on South Congress Avenue. The flood knocked out the power plant and turned the city's drinking water to an unsafe silty brown liquid.

The flood, sweeping wreckage along with it, crashed on down the river. Bastrop, Smithville, La Grange, Columbus, Wharton. No community was spared as the muddy, swirling water raced toward Matagorda Bay.

Because the house at 1611 was on high ground, Mary Elizabeth and her family were never in danger. But it was several days before they had drinking water and lights again.

Mary Elizabeth eagerly read accounts of the flood in the *Austin American.* These were real stories written by real newspaper reporters. She noted the bylines: Lorraine Barnes, Raymond Brooks, Charles E. Green, Weldon Hart, Ruth Lewis, William J. Weeg. Someday, she promised herself, she would be a newspaper reporter. She would see her own name in a byline on a front-page story.

On January 20, 1937, President Roosevelt was inaugurated for his second term. For many years, March 4 had been Inauguration Day. The Twentieth Amendment to the Constitution, often called the "lame duck" amendment, changed the date.

As the 1930s drew to a close, the Depression eased. Many of President Roosevelt's New Deal programs, plus the growing threat of war in Europe, had created more jobs. Tom Sutherland was now working steadily on his road construction work. He favored an informal method of doing business. He often kept his financial records on slips of paper and backs of envelopes stuffed in his pockets. A simple handshake, he said, was as good as a written contract.

One afternoon Mary Elizabeth came home from school and discovered a dirty, asphalt-clotted old truck parked at 1611 West Avenue.

Her cheeks flaming with embarrassment, Mary Elizabeth stormed into the house. "Whose old wreck is that in front of this house?" she demanded.

Her father and his construction foreman, C. M.

Patton, had come in off the road that afternoon. "That's *my* truck, Missy!" the foreman said. "Without it you wouldn't eat."

George began to spend his summers as Tommy had — working on road construction with his father. Young as he was, George was soon driving his daddy's Pontiac from site to site. He learned to manage the business. And he started an unusual hobby: collecting empty whiskey bottles.

When George came home from West Texas, he brought a carload of empty bottles of all different sizes, shapes, and colors. Mary Elizabeth bcame interested in the collection. The two children discovered that the university area, particularly the morning after a football game, was a great hunting place.

They stashed their collection in the old carriage house behind 1611. Mary E occasionally viewed the growing assortment with a sigh of bewilderment. A lifelong Methodist and a nondrinker, she couldn't understand the fascination with empty bottles. As long as her children weren't the ones who emptied them, she reckoned there was no harm in it.

By the time Mary Elizabeth completed University Junior High School, she had decided on her career. She wanted to be a journalist, a newspaperwoman — someone like the columnist Dorothy Thompson or Adela Rogers St. Johns, the Hearst reporter.

Even the First Lady, Mrs. Eleanor Roosevelt, described herself as a journalist. She wrote a daily newspaper column, "My Day." And she regularly sold articles to leading magazines. Mrs. Roosevelt was the most popular woman in the United States, and Dorothy Thompson was second.

Mary Elizabeth wanted to travel the world and make it her "beat." She could hardly wait to finish high school and follow Tommy and Alice to the university.

Austin High School, at 1212 Rio Grande, was not far from the house at 1611. From the campus Mary Elizabeth had a clear view of the pink granite Texas Capitol.

Instead of filling out cards or standing in lines to sign up for classes, students at Austin High School ran for them. On the first day of each semester they raced through the halls, hoping to get permission from their favorite teachers for the classes they wanted.

Mary Elizabeth threw her boundless energies into all her high school classes — even home economics. One day she brought home a recipe for coffee cake. She mixed and baked it without any help from Alice or her mother. The cake certainly didn't turn out as she had expected.

"Are you sure you followed the recipe exactly?" Mary E asked. "What are all these dark brown specks?"

"Oh, that's the cup of coffee the recipe called for," Mary Elizabeth said. It was then that she realized she had made the mistake of using ground coffee instead of the brewed liquid. The family tactfully set the cake aside without further comment.

George was working after school as a Senate page in the Capitol. He often came home late, tired, and hungry. That night he was surprised and delighted to find a whole cake on the table in the darkened kitchen. He gobbled it up, washed it down with some cold milk, and went to bed full and happy.

"I'm surprised you were able to sleep at all, eating a whole cup of coffee grounds," his cousin Malcolm teased him the following morning.

Mary Elizabeth enrolled in journalism classes in high school. Her teacher, James W. Markham, encouraged her. He came by the house one evening to ask Mary E's permission to take Mary Elizabeth on an interscholastic journalism trip to Abilene in West Texas. As soon as he seated himself on the living room couch, he shouted out in pained surprise. He reached back and withdrew a kitchen knife from among the cushions.

"Oh, so that's where my knife has been," Mary E said as she accepted it from him. Someone in the crowded house, perhaps paring fruit or cutting a chunk of cheese, had carelessly left the knife on the couch.

Mary Elizabeth spent as much time as she could in the third-floor offices of the *Maroon,* the high school newspaper. The typewriters and the horseshoe-shaped desk made her imagine she was in a real newspaper office. Movies such as *Front Page,* with Pat O'Brien as a reporter, had given her an imaginative idea of what to expect from a career as a journalist.

Her friend, Patti Nolen, was editor of the *Comet,* the school's yearbook. Like her sister Alice before her, Mary Elizabeth was chosen editor of the *Maroon.* Leslie Carpenter, a tall, slender boy, was business manager of the *Maroon.*

Mary Elizabeth and Leslie quickly became friends. Soon Leslie was among the many young people who came by 1611 after school several times a week.

"I've been thinking about that story," he might say, making his way from the front door to the kitchen cabinet. "I think we can add some jokes, make it a little funnier." He would help himself to a peanut butter sandwich as he talked.

Mary Elizabeth and Leslie enjoyed collaborating, especially on humorous writing projects. If one thought of a gag or a pun, the other quickly topped it. Finally they would collapse with laughter, almost unable to continue.

"I'm glad you have a nice young man to study with dear," Mary E observed. "I just hope my supply of peanut butter holds out until you graduate."

8. The Eyes of Texas

"Hey, Liz!"

"Hi, Liz. How ya doin'?"

Mary Elizabeth Sutherland quickly grew accustomed to her new name. *Liz* sounded brisk, crisp — no time wasted. The name suited her own energetic personality and the purposeful atmosphere of the University of Texas campus in 1938.

Freshmen Liz Sutherland and Les Carpenter were among 10,000 students enrolled in the university that year. Most of the students lived in their homes or in boardinghouses near the campus.

Many of the buildings were new. The U.T. Tower had been completed in 1937.

Homer Price Rainey, an outspoken champion of academic freedom, was the university's president. Walter Prescott Webb taught history, J. Frank Dobie taught English, and DeWitt Reddick taught journalism.

Liz and Les enrolled in all the journalism courses they could fit into their schedules. They spent much of their free time in the offices of the school newspaper, *The*

Daily Texan, in the Journalism Building. They took on any writing job they found.

In her junior year Liz pledged the Alpha Phi sorority. She formed friendships and loyalties that were to last a lifetime. Liz continued to live at home, but the Alpha Phi house at 2005 University Avenue became a daytime campus home.

Les was night editor of *The Daily Texan* for three years. In 1940 he was humor editor and later associate editor of the *Texas Ranger,* a popular campus magazine. He was also a member of the selection committee that chose the "Girl of the Month." Not surprisingly, Mary Elizabeth Sutherland was selected October's Girl of the Month.

Even then Les couldn't resist a joke. Most of the pictures of the Girl of the Month were full-page, glamorous studio portraits. In the October issue, the top photograph was a gag shot with a mock cutline. Below that one, Liz's photograph was identified as "Alpha Phi runner-up."

Liz dated other boys and Les dated other girls. But it was obvious to anyone who saw the two together they shared many common goals and interests. They had a deep friendship and a growing romantic attraction.

With her love of politics, Liz was delighted to find that the campus offered opportunities to campaign for office.

"I'm going to run for vice president of the Students' Association," she announced to her sorority sisters. "A girl's never been elected. I think it's high time."

Her flyers announced her qualifications: Orange Jackets, Wesley Foundation Cabinet, *Daily Texas* Editorial Board, Theta Sigma Phi (honorary journalism society), and the Round-Up Committee.

Liz ran against two young men, E. A. (Buddy) Givens and Jimmy Craig, both with unlimited imaginations and funds to match. Jimmy even offered his supporters free rides in his private airplane. Liz countered with the slogan: "Keep Your Feet on the Ground with Sutherland."

In her statement of candidacy Liz said: "I don't ask you to vote for me BECAUSE I'm a girl or IN SPITE of the fact I'm a girl. I only ask you to base your choice on the person you sincerely believe will make the most EFFECTIVE vice president."

The election took place near Easter. Liz and her sorority supporters displayed a mother duck and her babies in a cage along the main mall. They put up a big banner: "Duck in and Vote for Liz."

Liz won the election.

Although Liz was fascinated by politics on any level, her main love was journalism. She believed that as a journalist she could go anywhere, see everything, ask anybody any questions.

"A press card," Dr. Reddick told her, "is your passport to the world."

Her sister, Alice, graduated from the university in August 1939. Alice was soon planning her wedding to John Romberg. Unlike her brother's wedding in 1933, Alice wanted a traditional ceremony. She wore her mother's wedding gown and carried a prayer book that had belonged to her great-grandmother. Tommy's oldest daughter, four-year-old Carol, was the flower girl.

Liz was maid of honor. She wore powder blue and carried pink rosebuds. Leslie, an usher, couldn't have failed to notice how lovely she looked.

Liz and Les always enjoyed plays and movies. They went to see *His Girl Friday.* The 1940 movie was a remake of the 1931 film, *Front Page.* The new movie starred Rosalind Russell as Hildy Johnson. The playwrights, Ben Hecht and Charles MacArthur, originally wrote the Johnson role for a male actor. Liz thought the substitution a perfectly natural one. She saw no reason why a woman couldn't be a front-page reporter.

As she sat in the darkened movie theater, absorbed in the fast-paced and snappy dialogue, Liz pictured herself perched on the corner of the city editor's desk, pushing her hat back with an impatient gesture, and exchanging wisecracks with the other reporters.

Sunday afternoon, December 7, 1941, Les and Liz were at one of their favorite meeting places, the Triple X Famous Foods, 2801 Guadalupe, enjoying hamburgers and frosted root beers.

The *Austin Sunday American* newspaper was propped between them. Saturday's football victory was the lead story. Beneath a five-column photograph, the headline boasted: "Longhorns Shatter Oregon by 71–7." Coach Dana X. Bible and his team had given the University of Texas a football victory that would be remembered and talked about for years.

Inside were more football photos, as well as advertisements to entice Christmas shoppers. The weather had been so mild — up to 75 degrees just a day or so ago — that no one could get in much of a Christmasy mood.

Les and Liz thought about going to the movies. The Paramount Theater listed *Sergeant York,* starring Gary Cooper. Cooper played the role of Alvin York, a World War I infantryman who had earned the Medal of Honor for his action against German soldiers in 1918. The movie sounded depressing. There was already too much talk of war. Besides, the afternoon was too nice to waste indoors. If they wanted something to do, they could help their friends put the finishing touches on the booths for the next day's Varsity Carnival.

Walter Nixon, a university journalism student and a writer for the *Ranger,* rushed into the Triple X, a look of disbelief on his face. He came straight to the table where Liz and Les sat.

"The Japanese have bombed Pearl Harbor," he said. "I just heard it on my car radio."

"Where's Pearl Harbor?" Liz asked.

"I'm not sure," Les replied. "But it doesn't sound good."

Other customers began talking anxiously. Pearl Harbor? Is it ours? Does this mean war? No, can't be. Says right here, peace talks continuing. Isn't some Japanese ambassador in Washington?

Soon the cries of "EX-tra, EX-tra!" confirmed their fears. The university's football victory was swept from the front page. In banner headlines, the *Austin Sunday American* proclaimed: "Japs Attack U.S. Harbors in Hawaii and Philippines."

Ordinarily, Liz looked forward to Sunday night radio. She enjoyed Jack Benny, followed by Charlie McCarthy and Edgar Bergen. "One Man's Family" was her favorite. That night, however, the people at 1611 West Avenue waited with impatience until 8:00 to hear what Walter Winchell had to say.

"Good evening, Mr. and Mrs. North America and all the ships at sea," Winchell began as usual. He was known as "America's number-one newsboy." His breezy style and show-business slang had made his newspaper columns and radio commentaries popular across the country.

That night's news, however, was grim and somber.

The following Monday the *Austin American* hit the streets with another extra edition.

Almost everyone, it seemed, gathered around radios to listen to President Roosevelt speak to the nation from the White House in Washington. He spoke in a calm, deliberate voice, spacing his words for emphasis. He described December 7 as "a date which will live in infamy." Grimly, he listed the targets that had been attacked: Hawaii, Guam, the Philippines. He concluded: "I ask that the Congress declare that since the unprovoked and dastardly attack by Japan on Sunday, December 7, 1941, a state of war has existed between the United States and the Japanese Empire."

Lines quickly formed outside recruiting offices all over the country as young men rushed to sign up for military service. Many of Liz and Les's friends on campus entered the ROTC. Les joined the Naval Reserve Officer Training Corps. The program allowed him to complete his college degree while receiving naval training.

The entire university quickly mobilized for the war effort. The school adopted a year-round curriculum and began offering more courses in sciences, engineering, and foreign languages.

George left the university at midterm. He went to Lubbock, where he could study at Texas Tech while helping his father in the construction business.

Tom Sutherland had almost more work than he could handle. Instead of building roads for Texas, he was building airfield landing strips for the United States.

Liz's brother, Tommy, had accepted a job with the newly created Board of Economic Warfare, headed by Vice President Henry Wallace. The BEW's task was to obtain strategic war materials from foreign sources. Tommy and his wife, Lois, and their daughters packed up and moved to Washington.

By 1942 the "state of war" Roosevelt spoke of had changed civilian life noticeably. In January, Austin participated in its first practice blackout. Soon scarce products, such as sugar, coffee, and gasoline, were available only in exchange for ration coupons.

Everyone had a role to play and a contribution to make to the war effort. Schoolchildren participated in fitness programs, bought Savings Stamps, and collected tinfoil and scrap metal. Women saved fat and grease from their kitchens. They met in neighborhood groups to roll bandages for the Red Cross or knit scarves and socks for men in the services. Families were encouraged to provide additional food by growing Victory Gardens in their backyards.

Liz and Les were in the last few months of their senior year. They lugged a typewriter to a popular campus hangout. There they collaborated on a musical comedy, "Time Staggers On," a competition play sponsored by Theta Sigma Phi. The title was a takeoff on the newsreel, "The March of Time," which always concluded with the words "Time marches on."

"Don't say anything funny around Liz and Les," Sue Kone warned their campus friends. "They'll put it in their script."

When time came for dress rehearsals, Les refused to let their friends attend. "Oh, no," he said. "We don't want you to know how many gags we've stolen from you."

Liz and Les won $25 for their entry. Their play was produced in Hogg Auditorium February 11 and 12, 1942. The play raised enough money for the Theta Sigs to purchase a $100 war bond.

Work on the play offered only brief distraction from the war. Every day headlines, radio reports, and newsreels reminded the seniors of the pressure to graduate — to get out and do something for the war effort. The Class of 1942 became more and more excited as graduation day approached.

On Tuesday, June 2, 1942, Mary Elizabeth Sutherland received her bachelor of journalism diploma. Mary E, filled with pride at her daughter's many accomplishments at the university, saw to it that Liz had a white gardenia corsage to wear.

Les left Austin to attend the U.S. Naval Reserve Midshipman's School at Columbia University in New York City.

After the excitement of graduation, Liz gathered the clippings of her published writings into a scrapbook. Her journalism professor, Dr. DeWitt Reddick, encouraged her in her career choice. Just as well, because she had never seriously considered anything else. She had wanted to be a newspaperwoman, a journalist, as far back as she could remember.

Liz had an idea. "Let's get a used car and travel all over Texas writing feature stories," she suggested to her friends Jean Begeman and Elizabeth Wharton. "I know we can at least make our expenses, and think what fun it would be!"

The young women located a used hearse available for $100. Perhaps not the most cheerful setting for a roving newsroom, but at least it had plenty of space for their typewriters.

The more they thought about it, the more exciting

the plan became. And the less practical. World War II had created shortages in almost every area. Rubber for tires and gasoline for nonessential travel were in short supply. Reluctantly, the women abandoned their notion.

Liz wasn't sure exactly what else she might want to do, but she was sure of one thing. "I won't go to Washington," she firmly told her family. "Everyone there is just trying to pull a hunk of personal glory from the national garbage can!"

Mary E laughed out loud. "My kingdom," she said. "Is this the same daughter who told me she'd have given anything to be in Washington in 1917, because it was so exciting with a world war going on and so many Texans in positions of influence? But that's all right," her mother added. "You don't have to decide your whole future this very minute. Why don't you go to Houston and visit your Aunt Alice? She's so proud of you. I know she'd love to see you."

Liz had visited in her aunt's Houston home two or three times. She never overcame her sense of awe. The home of Alice and her husband, Jim West, Jr., at 1909 River Oaks Boulevard, was so *spacious*. Liz was used to big houses: the Robertson home in Salado, even 1611 West Avenue. But those houses were always tumbling full of relatives. The West home almost echoed with emptiness.

Alice Robertson West was delighted to have her young niece visit her. She was eager to help further Liz's career plans. She bought Liz a new wardrobe suitable for a young woman leaving the campus and entering the business world.

"If you want to attend Northwestern University for a master's degree this fall, Jim and I will help," Aunt Alice said. "But you don't have to decide now. Meanwhile, why don't you go to Washington, just for a visit? Who knows? You might like it."

As Liz left the West home, her uncle tucked four crisp, new hundred-dollar bills in her pocket.

9. Miss Liz Goes to Washington

The modern Houston Municipal Airport was only a year old in 1942. The place hummed with activity. Liz began to feel excited in spite of her misgivings about Washington. Then she saw the plane she was to board.

She took one terrified look at the twenty-one-seat DC-3 commercial airplane. She realized immediately this contraption defied all the laws of God and gravity. Her brother George, a qualified pilot, loved to fly. Staring at this plane, Liz couldn't see the attraction.

Did anyone expect her to believe those two flimsy propellers on the front were powerful enough to keep that big, heavy heap of metal up in the air? The plane looked no more dependable to her than one of her younger brother Billy's balsa wood and rubber band toys.

The clickety-clack and gentle swaying of a train were pleasant childhood memories. The sudden dips and lurches of the airplane were terrifying to Liz. She planted both feet firmly on the metal floor, drew her arms in close to her sides, and clutched her small handbag with white-knuckled fingers.

Liz's attempts at polite conversation with her seatmate did little to relieve her fear of flying. Many of her fellow passengers were service men and women — another reminder that she was on her way to the capital of a nation at war.

Virginia Howell Holloman, a first cousin about Tommy's age, met Liz at the New Orleans airport. "How was your flight?" her cousin asked.

"I'm exhausted," Liz admitted. "I've been holding the plane up since Houston!"

Virginia laughed. "You'll get used to flying."

"Never!" Liz swore.

Virginia was eager to share the historic sights of New Orleans with her cousin. Liz enjoyed her all too short visit. She dreaded boarding the plane again, but by now she was beginning to look forward to Washington.

It was simply a case of love at first sight, as Liz later wrote in her book, *Ruffles and Flourishes.* She risked a glance out the window as the plane banked for its landing. Even in wartime, the city twinkled "like a necklace of diamonds along the black ribbon of the Potomac."

Tommy met his sister at the airport and drove her into the city. Liz was captivated by the Lincoln Memorial. Tommy drove around it twice while she craned for a better view. Finally he parked the car and Liz raced up the stairs of the white marble building.

Spotlights usually illuminated the large statue of a seated, brooding Abraham Lincoln. But wartime Washington was blacked out because of the threat of enemy bombing. On the wall above the figure was the inscription:

> In this temple as in the hearts of the people for whom he saved the Union the memory of Abraham Lincoln is enshrined forever.

Later that evening Tommy sent a telegram to their mother:

June 11, 1942

Mrs. T. S. Sutherland
1611 West Avenue
Austin, Texas

Mary Elizabeth has arrived safe much love to you the day after your birthday we are all well. Tell Daddy hello. Having hot weather. Tommy.

Tommy and his wife, Lois, had a large house in nearby Kensington, Maryland. Even with their four daughters, Carol, Barbara, Gayle, Beth, and the two-month-old baby, Kay, there was still plenty of room for Liz to stay.

Liz was shocked to see so many women wearing slacks in public! War certainly changed things. "Don't you know there's a war on?" people said as the reason or excuse for everything.

Washington was filled with thousands of "government girls," as they were called. Most men were in the service, so women worked in the many federal offices. Liz soon took her place among them.

She worked part-time in the office of Creekmore Fath from Austin. Fath, like Liz, had worked on the Austin High School *Maroon* and was a University of Texas graduate. He was counsel to the Senate Committee on Patents. The work involved getting essential war materials. Although Liz did some editing, her job didn't call for writing.

"This," she told her brother and sister-in-law one evening, "is not the career I had in mind. I came here to be a journalist."

One day Drew Pearson, a well-known Washington columnist, came into the patent office. "I don't believe I've seen you before," he said to Liz. "Are you one of the new press girls?" That's what Pearson called women journalists.

Creekmore Fath's secretary, Edith Connally, knew some press bureau people. She offered to help Liz meet them. So Liz grabbed her scrapbook of byline clips and headed for the National Press Building. All of the major newspapers and magazines had offices there for their Washington staff.

Liz started knocking on doors. Esther Van Wagoner Tufty opened one of those doors. Esther Tufty was tall — almost six feet — and regal in appearance, with her coronet of heavy braids. Everyone called her "Duchess." She had come to Washington and established the Tufty News Service in 1935. Now, at forty-six, the Duchess ran a news bureau serving two dozen Michigan newspapers. She also was a member of the five-person accreditation committee for Mrs. Roosevelt's women press correspondents group.

Liz showed Esther Tufty her clips. The Duchess was impressed with Liz's eagerness and her ambition to be a newspaperwoman.

"There's still a lot of prejudice against women journalists," Tufty explained. "Most newspapers hire women only to do society page news or to write sob sister stories. The war, with so many men away in service, has given women opportunities they'd never have had otherwise," she continued. "But Eleanor Roosevelt has caused more to be written by, for, and about women than anyone else."

News stories about Eleanor Roosevelt after the 1932 election described her as a "new kind of First Lady." She considered herself a working journalist. She earned money selling articles to newspapers and magazines.

Eleanor Roosevelt held the first press conference called for a president's wife. Mrs. Roosevelt's close friend, Associated Press reporter Lorena Hickok, suggested having press conferences for women reporters only.

"Unless women reporters can find something new to write about, the chances are many of them will lose their jobs," Lorena Hickok explained.

Mrs. Roosevelt liked the idea. March 6, 1933, just two days after President Roosevelt's inauguration, she met with a group of thirty-five women reporters, or "press girls," as they were called.

"I'll see you all again once a week," Mrs. Roosevelt told them.

When the Duchess hired Liz as a reporter, she arranged for Liz to be accredited to Mrs. Roosevelt's press correspondents.

The First Lady's press conferences were social. The press girls wore hats and gloves and were offered tea.

From the edge of the group, Liz stretched on tiptoes for a glimpse of the First Lady. She was quite tall, perhaps close to six feet, Liz guessed. She wore a rather shapeless dress of a shade called "Eleanor blue." But it was the woman's voice that Liz and others noticed first. Her voice was high-pitched and a little wavery. Her comments were often punctuated by giggles.

Liz soon came to respect the First Lady for her graciousness, her close attention, and her sincere desire to promote women.

Mrs. Roosevelt liked to use her press conferences to help women in office or women with causes. Over a period of time, Liz became well acquainted with a number of them. Frances Perkins was the first woman to be secretary of labor and a cabinet member. Molly Dewson was head of the Women's Division of the National Democratic Committee. Mary McLeod Bethune was a well-known black teacher. She was Negro affairs director for the National Youth Administration.

Liz's work as a reporter led her to call on the offices of Texans in Washington. One was Oveta Culp Hobby, commander of the Women's Army Corps (WAC). Mrs. Hobby, the wife of former Texas Governor William Hobby, had been the first woman parliamentarian of the Texas House of Representatives. FDR had asked her to come to Washington in May 1942 to form a women's auxiliary. The idea was that women could perform many noncombat jobs.

Liz, like many Americans, had not yet had time to adjust to the idea of women serving in the army.

"I have to tell you, I'm not a WAC-er," Liz blurted.

In her khaki uniform and her visored cap, Colonel Hobby was a model of crisp efficiency. She arched her finely groomed eyebrows. "Well," she said coolly, "a white feather for you." Then she proceeded with the interview.

Liz also called on the office of her congressman from the Tenth District, Lyndon B. Johnson. As a Naval Reserve officer, Johnson was on active duty and was away on an inspection tour. His wife, Lady Bird Johnson, kept the congressional office open and maintained contact with the constituents.

Mrs. Johnson was a slender, dark-haired young woman with brown eyes and a warm smile. Her East Texas accent was overlaid, Liz detected, with tones of the deeper South.

Liz and Lady Bird became friends from the start. Liz found herself telling Lady Bird about her journalism degree from the University of Texas.

"I have a degree in journalism from the university too," Lady Bird Johnson responded. She tilted her head and smiled. "I always thought people in the press went more places and met more interesting people, and more interesting things happened to them."

"Oh, me too," Liz said, laughing. "I used to read Richard Halliburton's books and dream of visiting the Taj Mahal."

For the time being, at least, Liz's reporting assignments were not quite that romantic.

Liz was disappointed that John Nance Garner, vice president from 1933 to 1941, had returned to his home in Texas. "Been away from my fishing too long," he had said by way of farewell to Washington.

Gone but not forgotten, the Duchess and Ruby Black assured Liz. "You can still smell the cabbage," they joked.

Garner and his wife, Ettie, never entered Washington's social life. They lived in three rented rooms in Hotel Washington and did most of their own cooking. Cactus Jack, as the Washington press called him, was fond of cabbage, lamb chops, and pickled pigs' feet. He also smoked cigars. The aromas, Washingtonians insisted, lingered on.

Liz quickly became friends with Washington newswomen. Ruby Black, she learned, was a Texan. She had been the first woman ever to serve as editor-in-chief of *The Daily Texan.* She won the National Headline Award in 1941. She resigned from United Press in 1942 to become a full-time publicist.

Ruth Cowan was another ex-University of Texas journalism student in Washington. She had covered the Texas legislature for United Press. Ruth often used the byline "R. Baldwin Cowan" because of the prejudice against women reporters. In 1943 she was accredited by Associated Press and covered WAC units overseas.

Liz was soon attending press conferences, reporting on Congress, interviewing Speaker of the House Sam Rayburn of Texas, and getting an insider's view of Washington and politics. For all of this, Liz now earned $25 a week.

Encouraged by such a large, regular salary, Liz looked around for an apartment. She urged her friends, Sue Kone, Eugenia Worley, and Penny Chatmas, to join her in Washington. They quickly became government girls. Sue went to work for the War Production Board. Eugenia worked for the Weather Bureau, charting weather maps at the national airport. Their roommate, Cynthia Sheffield, was a lieutenant in the Navy.

The girls shared their ration coupons, expenses, and household chores. Liz also shared the excitement of her work as a news reporter. She told them about her interview with Charles MacArthur, author of *Front Page* and husband of the actress Helen Hayes. Liz often burst into the apartment, eager to relate the big stories of the day.

One afternoon she was solemn, almost tearful. "The president can't stand up," she told her friends.

Most Americans knew FDR had suffered from polio, or infantile paralysis as it was called, in 1923. Few realized he had never recovered use of his legs. The young women, now in their early twenties, had grown up seeing newspaper photographs and newsreels of a jaunty, confident, apparently vigorous president. He always was shown seated or covered behind a lectern or podium. The photographs did not reveal President Roosevelt's wasted, paralyzed legs.

The girls loved living in Washington. There was just one hitch: Only married women were permitted to lease apartments. One of their friends from the university, Patti Nolen, was now Mrs. Forest B. Crain. She agreed to show her marriage license and let her name appear on the lease. The girls named their apartment the Bedside Manor.

When the landlord or the Civil Defense block captain came around asking for Mrs. Crain, the roommates blithely said, "Oh, she's out shopping. Can't one of us take care of it for her?"

That ruse soon wore thin. Liz and Eugenia voted Sue Kone the person most able to pull off a masquerade with a straight face. She bought a cheap wedding ring from a dime store. As a "married woman" she wore the ring when she paid the rent.

10. Navy Bride

On her twenty-second birthday, September 1, 1942, Liz came back to the apartment from work and found a small package from Les. She shook the box and tried to guess its contents. What could it be? Eagerly she tore into the wrapping, then sat back in surprise.

Sue Kone came into the room and noted her friend's stunned expression.

"What is it, Liz?" Sue asked. "What's happened?"

"I'm not sure," Liz answered. "I think I've just been proposed to, sort of."

Liz showed Sue six silver teaspoons nested in tissue paper and read aloud the enclosed note:

> Dear Liz:
>
> I started to have a *C* engraved on them but I decided against it for two reasons . . . I didn't know whether you'd like it and . . . I might not come back [from the war].
>
> Les

Liz and Les wrote a flurry of letters back and forth.

They visited each other when wartime travel restrictions allowed. Les Carpenter was commissioned as an ensign in June 1943 and assigned to a patrol boat based at Key West, Florida.

In September 1943 Les surprised Liz again — this time with an engagement ring.

"I know if I don't marry him," Liz confided to her roommates, "I'll always feel I missed the boat."

The young ensign wrote to Liz's mother in Austin, formally asking permission to marry Liz. He waited an agonizing three weeks for her reply.

Mary E was proud of Liz's accomplishments. Based on the experiences of women of her own generation, she was afraid marriage would put an end to Liz's dreams of a career in journalism. She set aside her reservations, however. She promised to keep peanut butter in the refrigerator for Les's visits and wished the engaged couple her "most heartfelt wishes for lasting happiness."

Even in wartime, there was much to do to get ready for the wedding.

"I'm going home this fall," Liz told Sue Kone. "You want to go with me?"

The two young women came up with a plan for getting a car. Servicemen leaving from Washington for overseas duty often arranged for someone to drive their cars back home. Senator Tom Connally of Texas knew a man who needed someone to drive his car to Palestine in East Texas. If the girls got that far, they would manage the remaining distance somehow. Liz crammed every box and suitcase she could into the car, and the two set off.

Liz was driving as they chatted eagerly, happy to be in Texas again and delighted with the idea of spending Christmas at home. Suddenly, *bang!* One of the tires, worn to the threads and irreplaceable due to wartime shortages, blew out. Liz fought the swerve and braked too hard. The car left the narrow road and thumped into an adjacent farm field.

Badly shaken but not seriously injured, the two tried

to figure out what to do next. They needed to notify the dealer in Palestine, who was expecting the car. They had to find some other way to get to Austin. Perhaps they could walk to the nearest phone, but what on earth could they do with all those suitcases?

Fortunately, the motorist who came to their aid was the father of one of their former Austin High School classmates.

Finally, they reached Austin. Not to the old, familiar 1611 West Avenue, but to Mary E's new home at 1900 Forest Trail.

At Christmas Les wired a dozen red roses to Liz. Liz announced her engagement on December 29 in a mock newspaper format, the "Marital Messenger." Three of brother Tommy Sutherland's daughters, Carol, Barbara, and Gayle, dressed in matching newsboy outfits and passed them out.

Liz soon was caught up in a swirl of social activity. She was honored with teas, luncheons, and showers, in keeping with the traditions of the time. Mrs. Homer P. Rainey, wife of the former president of the University of Texas, and Mrs. DeWitt Reddick, wife of Liz and Les's beloved journalism professor, were among the many hostesses.

Liz's younger brother, George, had married his university sweetheart, Jean Taber, the previous year. Their first child, George Robertson Sutherland, Jr., was barely two months old when Liz revealed her plans, but Jean eagerly entered into the wedding preparations.

The wedding had been set for March. Three weeks before Liz's announcement, Les slipped and fell while aboard his patrol boat. His back injury kept him in a Navy hospital for five months.

Liz moved the date forward to June. Then she looked around for a job in Austin. She couldn't stand being idle. Besides, she wanted to earn money for her wedding expenses. She went to work as a reporter for the local newspaper where she and Les had both worked during their summers while at the university.

Liz skimmed through the morning newspaper, the *Austin American,* as she sat at her desk in the *Statesman* newsroom. The two newspapers shared a building at Seventh and Colorado streets.

The morning paper carried a regular syndicated column by Dorothy Thompson, one of Liz's favorite newspaperwomen. The *American* also ran articles by Liz's former professor, J. Frank Dobie, who was now in Cambridge, England.

The day was Ash Wednesday, February 23, 1944. Except for Liz and the city editor, Weldon Hart, the newsroom was deserted during the noon hour.

The bulletin bell on the news teletype machine began to ring. Hart ripped off a sheet of yellow paper, scanned the contents, and looked up. His eyes searched the room so earnestly that Liz turned to look behind her. Who could he be looking for?

"You," Hart said.

"Me?" Liz asked. She guessed from the editor's reluctance that he would have been happier giving the assignment to a more experienced reporter.

Hart quickly explained the bulletin. President Roosevelt's veto of a tax bill had angered Senator Alben Barkley of Kentucky. Barkley, the Senate majority leader, threatened to resign. The rift between the two could damage the Democratic party.

"I want you to go out and talk to some people," the editor said. "Get the local Democrats' reaction. Find out whose side they're on."

Liz grabbed her reporter's notebook and scampered out with a good deal more assurance than she actually felt. In spite of her experience working with the Duchess in Washington, she still thought of herself as a cub reporter.

But she did as she was told. Thursday afternoon's *Statesman* ran an Associated Press wire photo of Senator Barkley. Beneath the picture the headline proclaimed:

Austin Demos Think Dispute
Reaction Good
by Liz Sutherland

When Alben Barkley removed his finger from the

> break in the senatorial democratic dike, he did one of two things, according to Austin political strategists . . .

She had interviewed Texas Governor Coke Stevenson, Austin Mayor Tom Miller, and Miller's close political ally, attorney Edward Clark. It was a front-page political story, and she had earned a byline.

Mary E needn't have worried about Liz's marriage changing things. Nothing could have swerved Liz from her career goal now. She was hooked. There was no turning back.

Weldon Hart's interests were also turning to politics. He had been a sports editor, but with the *Statesman*'s managing editor Buck Hood away serving in the Marines, Hart had been shifted to the news desk.

A few days later a story appeared about the Campus League of Women Voters, based on an interview with Jane Cheatham of Waxahachie. This article did not bear Liz's byline, but it certainly carried her stamp. She may have written it:

> Austin would be knocked off its feet some day if a legion of Susan B. Anthonys stormed the state capitol to fight for some political measure . . .

After each day's newspaper was "put to bed," Liz joined other newspaper staffers at their favorite hangout. Hart, Lorraine Barnes, Ruth Lewis, and others gathered to talk shop. The lively exchange of news, gossip, and personal opinion continued Liz's journalism education begun in the classroom and on *The Daily Texan.*

While Liz remained behind to work for the *Statesman,* Sue Kone returned to the Washington apartment and her job at the War Production Board.

After his release from the hospital, Les had been reassigned from Key West to the Naval Public Information Office in Philadelphia. In June he rushed to Washington just long enough to get the marriage license — but Liz wasn't there.

"Don't worry," Sue told the distraught groom-to-be. "I'll go to the marriage license bureau with you. I can sign Liz's name as well as she can. No one will ever know the difference. And anyway, she'd do the same for me."

Sue not only signed the license, she made most of the other important arrangements for the wedding. She typed a checklist for Les so he wouldn't forget any detail.

Liz's aunt, Alice West, bought Liz's white marquisette wedding gown at Everitt-Buelow in Houston on June 9. Always filled with nervous energy, Liz fidgeted and squirmed through the necessary fittings. She managed to tear herself away from Texas' boiling political pot and get back to Washington on June 13. That same day Les wrote his commanding officer to "respectfully request three days leave" from the Navy, June 16 through June 19.

Liz and Les were married in a candlelight ceremony in a chapel of the National Cathedral in Washington on June 17, 1944. Guests from Texas, New York, and Washington included Congressman and Mrs. Lyndon Johnson.

Liz was a radiantly happy bride. Her brother, Tommy Sutherland, gave the bride away. Les, handsome in his white ensign's uniform, was attended by his friend Elgin Williams and his brother, John W. Carpenter, Jr.

Sue Kone was maid of honor and Penny Chatmas was bridesmaid. Sue waited until after the exchange of vows to tease her friend about the forged license. "I'm not sure you're legally married," Sue told Liz.

The couple spent their brief honeymoon in Hotel Pennsylvania in New York City. One evening they enjoyed seeing the comedian Milton Berle in a stage production of *The Ziegfeld Follies* at the Imperial Theatre. Even amidst the laughter they couldn't escape reminders of the war. The theater program carried a message from New York City's Mayor Fiorello LaGuardia: "in the event of an alert, remain in your seats, stay calm."

All too soon Les had to report back to duty. Philadelphia was crowded with service men and women and workers in plants manufacturing war materials.

The newlyweds were lucky to get their small apartment at 2311 Delancy Place. But Liz hated being alone so much of the day. She was used to a home crowded with relatives and friends, all talking at once, each sharing ideas and experiences. She had no tolerance for solitude.

Liz worked at being a good stay-at-home housewife as long as she could stand it — about two weeks.

"I've cooked every recipe in my *Better Homes* cookbook," she informed Les one evening. "I'm bored. I'm going back to work."

With her journalism credentials, Liz had no difficulty landing a job with United Press covering the Securities and Exchange Commission beat.

Usually she was able to rush back to the apartment and have lunch ready to share with Les. In the evenings the young couple enjoyed seeing plays or listening to speakers.

A few weeks after her own marriage, Liz was chosen to be matron of honor for her friend since second grade, Sue.

Sue turned her skill at planning weddings to her own use. On July 29 she discarded the fake wedding band she had used when paying the apartment rent on Bedside Manor and accepted a real ring from her new husband, Chester Drake.

Liz returned to her job in Philadelphia just in time to help cover a big story: the city's transit strike in August 1944.

The strike was triggered by racial conflict. Without the transit system, almost a million war workers were unable to get to their jobs. The strike could have crippled the war effort. President Roosevelt ordered armed soldiers into the city to halt the strike.

The war had touched the lives of almost everyone Liz knew. Tommy had left his office job to join the Navy. Liz's father, Tom, had suffered a stroke and George was running the construction business. Aunt Mabel had enlisted in the WAC.

That fall President Roosevelt, campaigning for a fourth term, toured Philadelphia. A popular campaign slogan was "Don't change horses in midstream," referring to the war effort.

No president of the United States had ever been elected to a fourth term. President Roosevelt's political advisers knew his chances would be improved if voters could be reassured about his health.

On a gray, rainy Friday, October 27, Liz saw President Roosevelt as he toured the city in an open car. That same evening she heard him speak to a crowd at Shibe Park.

"How did he look?" Les asked. Like many other Americans, he was afraid the war was too great a strain on the president. He might not live to complete another four years in office.

"Well, he just looked marvelous," Liz said. "He had on that old gray slouch hat he always wears and his Navy cloak thrown around his shoulders, and his cigarette holder at a jaunty angle. He waved and smiled at everyone."

Liz imitated FDR's familiar gestures, making Les laugh.

"But you know," Liz continued in a more serious tone, "I still remember the shock I felt the first time I saw him at a press conference in Washington. I came back to the apartment and told my roommates, 'The president of the United States can't even stand up.' "

Roosevelt won reelection on November 7, 1944. He defeated Thomas Dewey, Republican governor of New York. Roosevelt's running mate was Harry S. Truman, a senator from Missouri. Truman had been selected as the vice presidential candidate because he was acceptable to all parts of the Democratic party.

A few days after the national election, Liz received a note from Drew Pearson. He thanked her for the background material she had supplied on the dispute between Homer Rainey and the University of Texas Board of Regents. He said the information would appear in his next "Washington Merry-Go-Round" column.

Thursday, April 12, 1945, Les, Liz, and a fellow United Press reporter were having lunch and visiting in a Philadelphia tavern. Their waitress came to their table and said: "The president's dead."

They were stunned. Roosevelt had been president for twelve years. He had led the country out of the Depression and into the New Deal. With America's entry into World War II, he had become a strong international leader.

For a moment Liz and Les tried hard to remember the name of the new president. Truman. That was it. Harry Truman. He had only been vice president eighty-three days. No one seemed to know much about him, or what to expect from him as their new president.

Newspapers all over the nation soon hit the streets with extras. And as they had done on December 7, 1941, Americans gathered around their radios.

Even at the time of FDR's death, the war seemed to be nearing an end. Germany surrendered in May, and Japan surrendered August 14, 1945.

Les's back injury from his fall on the patrol boat had continued to bother him. With World War II at an end, he was soon able to apply for his discharge from the Navy.

Les and Liz didn't need to discuss their next step for long. They both wanted to go to Washington as journalists.

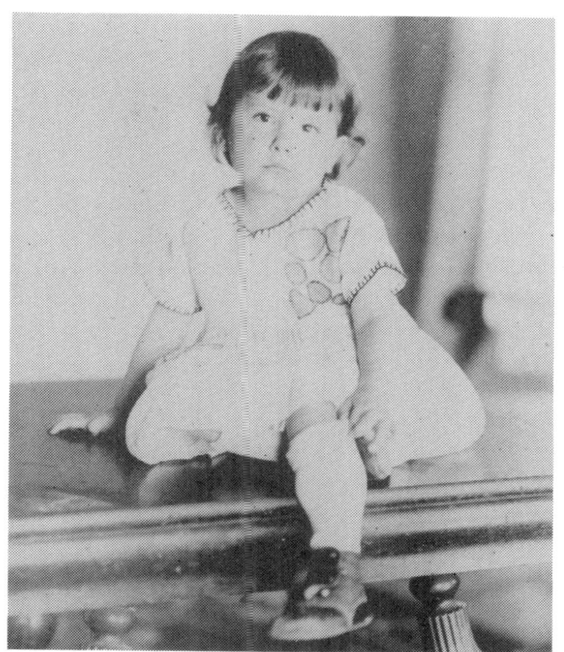

Three-year-old Mary Elizabeth Sutherland spent her summers and holidays at the Robertson home at Salado.

The Robertson home and grounds at Salado had plenty of room for Mary Elizabeth, her brothers and sister, and her many Robertson cousins.

Mary Elizabeth, shown here in her graduation picture, was editor of the Maroon, *student newspaper at Austin High School.* (Photo by Christianson Lieberman)

Mary Elizabeth and her friends shared an old jalopy, Petunia Bell.

Liz Sutherland, as she became known at the University of Texas, and her beau, Les Carpenter, at a prom in 1938.

Liz Sutherland (center) at her engagement announcement party. With her in the receiving line are Sue Kone, Penny Chatmas, and Navy Lt. (j.g.) Cynthia Sheffield.

Liz Sutherland was a radiantly happy bride as she became the wife of Ensign Les Carpenter. The ceremony took place in a chapel of the National Cathedral in Washington on June 17, 1944. (Photo by Underwood and Underwood, Washington, D.C.)

Washington was their beat as Liz and Les Carpenter reported the news of the nation's capital. (Photo by Del Ankers Photographers, Washington, D.C.)

Liz and her children, Christy and Scott, posed for a formal portrait in the Carpenters' "dream house," 4701 Woodway Lane. (Photo by Hessler Portraits, Washington, D.C.)

Scott Carpenter (left) and his sister Christy grew up in Washington, but Liz made sure her children knew their Texas heritage. (Photo by Johnny Bryson)

Christy and Scott Carpenter grew up in a home in which phone calls day and night signaled breaking news and Washington officials were frequent guests.

A beaming First Lady, Mamie Eisenhower, and Liz Carpenter, a proud mother, watch as President Eisenhower shakes hands with Scott and Christy Carpenter at the Women's National Press Club annual event in 1955.

The Women's National Press Club presented a Black Angus calf to President Dwight D. Eisenhower (left) for his Gettysburg farm. Senator Lyndon B. Johnson, Speaker of the House Sam Rayburn, and Liz Carpenter watch as President Eisenhower tries to attract the calf's attention. (Photo by Abbie Rowe)

Liz was the first woman to be appointed executive assistant to the vice president. From her office Liz helped coordinate the busy schedules of Lyndon and Lady Bird Johnson. (Photo by Rayt Lustig, *The Washington Star)*

News photographs of Lyndon Johnson lifting his beagles, Him and Her, by their ears got nationwide attention. Liz, as the First Lady's press secretary, jokingly posed in the White House doghouse with Him for photographers. (White House Photos)

With her journalism background, Liz was often called on to help write speeches. She is shown here with President Johnson working on the State of the Union message with presidential assistants Marvin Watson (left) and Joseph Califano (right).

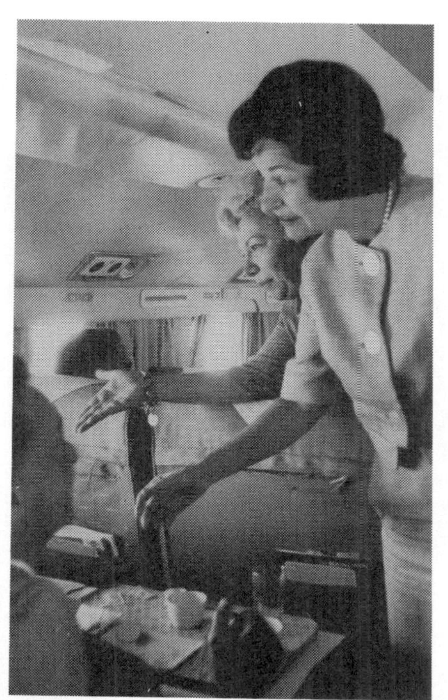

The First Lady and her press secretary visit with reporters on board one of their many flights. Mrs. Johnson shared Liz's dislike for flying but managed to conceal it with her gracious manner.

As press secretary and chief of staff for the First Lady, Liz goes over schedules with Lady Bird Johnson. Mrs. Johnson's favorite spot was a cozy sitting room in the West Wing of the White House.

Whether vacationing in an exotic clime (top) or recuperating in the hospital from emergency surgery, Liz demanded and got her typewriter. (Photo in hospital by Robert L. Knudsen, The White House)

Liz was a delegate to the International Year of the Woman conference in Copenhagen in 1980.

President Jimmy Carter asked Liz to come to Washington as assistant secretary of the newly created Department of Education.

"Grandma Whiz" hugs her grandson, Les Carpenter, son of Scott and Jean Carpenter.

At her Hill Country home, Grass Roots, Liz tends two whitetail fawns.

Liz demonstrates the proper technique for "Baying at the Moon."

Liz and Lady Bird Johnson have remained close friends and neighbors. They manage to travel together once or twice a year.

Bill Moyers dons an apron and prepares to pitch in for one of Liz's popular, informal parties.

First Lady Hillary Rodham Clinton (left) with Liz Carpenter and her daughter, Christy, at the Liz Carpenter Distinguished Lectureship, April 1993. (Photo by Larry Murphy, UT Austin News and Information)

11. Carpenter News Bureau

Les fell in love with Washington as quickly as Liz had. The nation's capital was a great place to be a newsman. He quickly found a job working for Bascom Timmons News Bureau in Washington.

If Liz expected to resume her place among the newswomen covering the First Lady, she was disappointed. Bess Truman made it clear she had no intention of holding press conferences.

One of Liz's friends from her university days, Jean Begeman, was in Washington. They hit on the scheme of writing a news column, "Southern Accents in Washington."

"We don't even need an office of our own to start out," Liz said. "Every office on our beat will have a typewriter we can use. We'll write our stories on the spot."

Working for themselves allowed the two women much more freedom than if they had worked for a newspaper or bureau. When Liz discovered she was pregnant, she was able to keep working.

Liz and Les were both delighted at the prospect of

becoming parents. "It's not something you have to think about," Liz said. "Children are the exclamation mark of love."

Mary E and George and Jean were in Denver visiting with Tommy when they received word that the baby was due.

Remembering her own difficult deliveries, Mary E wanted to be with her younger daughter. Mary E was sixty years old and had never flown, but she insisted on going to Washington as quickly as possible. George made the arrangements and helped his mother board the plane.

"In my day ladies came home to have their babies," Mary E told Liz. "But since there seems little prospect of that, I've come to Washington."

The couple's first child, Scott Sutherland Carpenter, was born September 9, 1946.

"I did all the work and you get the byline," Liz teased her husband.

Mary E stayed for a while, helping care for the baby. She sang the lullabies she had composed so many years ago for her own firstborn son. When Liz woke up in the mornings, she would tiptoe to the nursery and ease open the door. Mary E would often be asleep in the rocking chair with little Scott cradled in her arms.

Mary E's first plane trip was her last. When time came for her to leave Washington, she returned to Austin by train.

When she got home she told George and Jean about her frightening experience. "Everything was all right from Denver to St. Louis," she told her son and daughter-in-law. "But at St. Louis there was a terrible thunderstorm. My kingdom, but there was lightning everywhere!"

George, a pilot himself, tried to reassure his mother about commercial airline safety.

"Never mind all that," Mary E replied. "I know if you'd been at the controls during that storm, George, you'd never have taken off."

Liz's second pregnancy threatened to go on forever — and so did Congress.

"This baby's as slow as Christmas coming!" Liz said peevishly. "How can I keep on reporting for my newspapers? I'm getting bigger and bigger."

"You don't have to cover *every* story for your papers, honey," Les tried to tell her.

"Yes," she replied firmly. "I do."

Liz was covering news events on Capitol Hill. Finally, even the congressmen began to take note of Liz's condition. "If we don't adjourn soon," one member said, "we're liable to have a birth right here."

Mary E was unable to come to Washington this time. But brother Tommy was there. He took note of her immense size. "For God's sake, go home!" he said.

The baby was born December 15, 1949. She weighed seven pounds, seven ounces. She was named Christy for the Christmas season.

"Having babies while working as correspondent for a dozen newspapers is no way to grow old gracefully," Liz told her husband. Then, with a burst of her usual good humor, she added, "Rapidly, but not gracefully."

The following year, June 20, 1950, Mary E died at the home of her daughter, Alice Romberg, in Gonzales. That beautiful, intelligent, serene spirit was silenced. Liz never lost the memory. She carried it with her.

Les had been selling a number of freelance articles to magazines in addition to his work for Bascom Timmons. One of these, "The Whip from Texas," about Lyndon Johnson, appeared in *Collier's* magazine, February 1951.

Les and Liz already had such a close working partnership they decided to make it official. They opened the Carpenter News Bureau with offices at 812 National Press Building. They were news correspondents for newspapers in Texas, Oklahoma, and Arkansas.

The couple's friend from Austin, Buck Hood, helped them add the *Austin American-Statesman* to their list. They served several other Texas newspapers: *Abilene Reporter-News,* the *Amarillo Globe-Times,* the *Beaumont Enterprise* and *Journal,* and the *Houston Post.*

Les and Liz did what so many other couples did in the 1950s: They bought a house in the suburbs. Liz called the two-story rock house at 4701 Woodway Lane her "dream house."

The home was scarcely typical. Liz and Les were both working newspeople. Les often woke early. With his long-legged lope down the hill, he intercepted the carrier boy. He couldn't wait to see the morning newspaper. The phone rang constantly. Speaker Sam Rayburn and Lyndon Johnson were frequent guests in the Carpenter home.

In January 1953 the new United States senator from Texas, Price Daniel, and his wife, Jean, came to Washington. Soon they too were friends of the Carpenters.

Liz was chosen president of the Women's National Press Club. She began her duties June 1, 1954. As president, Liz introduced Queen Elizabeth, the Queen Mother, to members and dignitaries during Her Majesty's visit to Washington.

At thirty-four Liz was the youngest woman elected to head the Press Club, but not the first Texan. Her friend from the days of Mrs. Roosevelt's press conferences, Ruby Black, was the first. She had been followed by two other Texas women, Hope Riddings Miller of Sherman and Ruth Cowan of San Antonio. Ruth Montgomery, while not a native Texan, had studied at Baylor University in Waco.

Mamie Eisenhower, wife of President Dwight D. Eisenhower, elected in 1952, did not hold press conferences. Newswomen found other ways of getting information. They knew, for example, that a certain shade known as "Mamie pink" was the First Lady's favorite color. They knew she enjoyed spending the morning in bed. They knew she never missed her favorite soap opera, "As the World Turns."

The First Lady had a sense of humor. She didn't hesitate to laugh at herself. The newswomen planned a skit, "Mamie's Matinee," in which Mrs. Eisenhower was shown as the heroine of her own soap opera.

The president didn't always attend the annual Press Club event. Sometimes he sent the vice president or some other representative. This time Liz thought she had a good chance of getting President Eisenhower himself.

Even though he was in his first term, President Eisenhower already was looking forward to his retirement. He planned to be a "gentleman farmer" at his Gettysburg, Pennsylvania, home. He loved to invite people to his farm for barbecue.

Liz, herself the descendant of ranchers and stockmen, hit upon the idea of presenting him a calf for his farm.

"You don't mean a *real* one?" her colleagues asked.

"Well, of course a real one," Liz snapped. "That's the whole point."

Liz knew selecting the correct breed was important. She did some quick research. She enlisted the aid of friends at the Department of Agriculture.

"Why a Black Angus?" her assistant asked.

"Because they don't come in Mamie pink," Liz replied.

On the night of the presentation, Liz, dressed in a lovely new ballgown, herded a playful Black Angus calf backstage.

One of the waiters eyed the calf skeptically. "I've just planted some azaleas in my yard," he finally said. "May I have the fertilizer that calf's about to make?"

Liz arranged for two Texans, Speaker Rayburn and Lyndon Johnson, to make the formal presentation to the Texas-born Eisenhower. The calf remained well behaved. President Eisenhower was delighted with his gift. Young Scott and Christy had their picture taken shaking hands with the president.

Liz was selected as one of fourteen newswriters to tour Europe as part of a North Atlantic Treaty Organization project in 1956. Scott and Christy stayed with their aunt, Alice Romberg, in Gonzales.

After the official tour ended, Les joined Liz in Europe. They had been married a dozen years and were more in love than ever. Their travels together in Europe became a second honeymoon. Their first, in the midst of

World War II, had been much too brief.

Liz's friend from Austin, John Henry Faulk, had earned a reputation as a humorist. He had a popular New York radio show, "Johnny's Front Porch," and later "The John Henry Faulk Hour." Some people compared him to Will Rogers, the popular cowboy political humorist of the 1930s.

Liz was stunned when, in 1957, John Henry was fired by the radio network because of alleged Communist ties. During the "Cold War" of the 1950s, even an unproved hint of communism was enough to ruin a person. Many writers, artists, performers, and others were "blacklisted."

Tom Sutherland had never completely recovered from his stroke. He lived with his son and daughter-in-law, George and Jean Sutherland, in Austin for seven years. On April 3, 1957, he died at their home.

Liz wanted her children to know that even though they were born in Washington, their Texas roots were deep and strong. Whenever they could, Les and Liz returned to Texas for family visits.

Thanksgivings at Alice and John Romberg's home in Gonzales were always special occasions. They had a big house on a one-acre lot with towering old pecan trees and plenty of space for nieces and nephews. Dinners featured special dishes no one else could duplicate. Just the memory of Alice's grape and cream cheese salads and her pecan pie set mouths watering.

The Sutherlands and Robertsons were all great storytellers. Alice could hold her own against anyone. She and Tommy kept a heated competition going. Whenever they got together, each tried to outdo the other with tall tales.

Sadly, Alice never had the children she had longed for when she pretended she was bathing her babies. Alice served as Judge Romberg's secretary for thirty years. Some said it was Alice who "ran the courthouse."

On one visit to Austin, Liz showed ten-year-old Scott and seven-year-old Christy the names of their forebears in the Texas Capitol.

Former senator Price Daniel was now governor. Mrs. Jean Daniel, a descendant of Sam Houston, had a keen sense of the history of the Governor's Mansion. She invited the children to spend the night there. Scott stayed in the Sam Houston room.

Les and Liz enjoyed collaborating on plays. They wrote "My Unfair Ladies," for the annual dinner of the Women's National Press Club, May 16, 1957.

A preview in the *Washington Post* warned the skit would "startle the bejeepers" out of the politicians who attended.

This time President Eisenhower did not attend. He sent the vice president, Richard Nixon. The script included a big scene spoofing the vice president.

As the decade drew to a close, Liz took a moment to look back with satisfaction. She and Les had grown ever closer. They had two bright, attractive children. They had a home that was often filled with prominent people. Carpenter News Bureau was a success. She had earned recognition among her peers, the newswomen of Washington.

Her heart filled with gratitude and joy.

"I have everything any woman could possibly want," she said. "I can't even imagine living any other way. I don't want anything to change."

12. Our Great Adventure

The Carpenters' close friend, United States Senator Lyndon Johnson of Texas, announced his candidacy for president on July 5, 1960.

Les and Liz took their children, Scott and Christy, with them to Los Angeles for the Democratic National Convention on July 11. They wanted to cover the proceedings for the Carpenter News Bureau and to see if their friend would be chosen. They also wanted their children to learn how the nation's presidential candidates are selected.

The first business of a convention is the selection of a temporary chairman. The credentials committee seats the delegates and a permanent chairman is chosen. Then the hard work of drawing up a platform begins.

The highlight of the convention is the selection of the party's candidate. The chairman calls the roll of each state in alphabetical order. Nominations are made and seconded. Then voting begins.

Sometimes a number of ballots are needed before one person has a majority. In 1960, however, Senator John F. Kennedy was chosen on the first ballot.

Senator Kennedy selected Johnson as the person he wanted for the vice presidency.

"I don't think that Senator Johnson and I disagree on the great issues that face us," Kennedy said.

Lyndon Johnson occupied a very important position in the country as majority leader of the United States Senate. People wondered whether he would be willing to give that up to become vice president.

Traditionally the vice presidency carries very little power or prestige. Few vice presidents have had anything good to say about the job. John Nance Garner, the plain-talking Texan who had served eight years under President Franklin Roosevelt, said, "The vice presidency isn't worth a bucket of warm spit."

After Lyndon Johnson announced his acceptance, the Carpenters rushed to Chicago. There the Republican National Convention went through the same procedure. The Republicans chose Richard M. Nixon as their candidate for president. He selected Henry Cabot Lodge as his running mate.

Liz adored the spectacle of national conventions. She loved seeing the various delegates in some form of costume representing their home states. She especially enjoyed interviewing delegates who were attending a national convention for the first time. She found the colorful banners, the placards and balloons, the stirring music, the chattering and cheering and shouting very stimulating. And very exhausting.

After the conventions, Liz was enjoying a rare moment of relaxation when the phone rang. Lady Bird was calling from the LBJ Ranch in Texas.

After the first few moments of soft-spoken Southern courtesies, Lady Bird said, "Liz, Lyndon asked me to call you. He wants to know if you can take time off from your newspapers until after the election. We'd like you to share the great adventure of our lives."

Liz could hardly wait to tell Les. "The good news is LBJ wants me to join his campaign for vice president," she said.

"So what's the bad news?" Les asked, sensing a joke.

"The bad news is, I'll have to fly," Liz said. "You know how terrified I am of flying!"

Liz's family urged her to accept.

"You may hate flying," Les pointed out, "but you've always loved politics. Here's your chance to be really involved. You won't be looking on from the outside as a journalist. You'll be on the inside, helping make things happen."

"Besides," her fourteen-year-old son, Scott, added, "you'll be flying with Lady Bird. And who ever heard of a bird crash-landing?"

Liz had one last protest. "How will you get along without me at our news bureau?"

Her tall husband dropped an arm around her shoulder and gave her a quick squeeze. "I'll get along without you just fine. I'll just hire three people to replace you."

One of Liz's colleagues in the campaign was Bill Moyers, a young Baptist minister from Marshall, Texas, and a University of Texas graduate. He brouÿght a strong moral commitment to the campaign. Liz enjoyed working with him. His sense of humor and his quick skill with words made him a good partner for the many speeches the candidate needed.

Former President Harry Truman told Lyndon Johnson why he favored whistlestop campaigns. "Everybody knows where the train depot is," President Truman said. "You just let 'em know you're coming and they'll be down and listen to you."

Liz loved whistlestop campaigns. She enjoyed traveling through the country on the campaign train, stopping at small towns, and seeing the excited crowds. She would much rather be on a train than up in the air. Besides, the candidate could hardly make speeches from the back of an airplane.

Lyndon was right at home with the small-town crowds that gathered. In Culpepper, Virginia, just as the train was leaving, he shouted: "What has Dick Nixon ever done for Culpepper?"

"What has *anybody* ever done for Culpepper?" someone shouted back.

After Inauguration Day, January 20, 1961, Vice President Lyndon Johnson named Liz as his executive assistant. She was the first woman to hold such a post.

As vice president, Johnson served as president of the Senate. His offices were near the Senate floor.

Liz acted as liaison between Johnson and Mrs. Johnson, helping to coordinate their busy schedules. She also worked with the vice president's speechwriters. Although she was not Johnson's press secretary, she often helped arrange press conferences. Much of her time was spent on the offices' many telephones.

What got her down — or rather, up — was President Kennedy's desire to have Vice President Johnson represent the United States in visits to foreign countries. She couldn't use a White House limousine to go to Pakistan or India or any of the other countries overseas. She had to fly. But how exciting, to see the Taj Mahal and other romantic places she had read about as a child.

Liz quickly learned to toss a book of poetry or verse into her luggage. The slender volumes didn't take much space, and she could always count on them for a moment of inspiration or laughter.

In June 1961 Vice President and Mrs. Lyndon Johnson bought a house. The Elms, as it was called, had been the home of Mrs. Pearle Mesta, a well-known Washington hostess. Mrs. Johnson admired the gracious proportions of the house. She thought it would be perfect for the social duties expected of the vice president and his wife.

One of their guests that fall was Mrs. Eleanor Roosevelt. Mrs. Roosevelt had become known as the "First Lady of the World." When President Kennedy created the Presidential Committee on the Status of Women, he appointed Mrs. Roosevelt as the first chairperson. Esther Peterson, director of the Women's Bureau in the Labor Department, served as executive vice chairperson.

Liz was delighted to see Mrs. Roosevelt again, but she

was shocked by signs of the older woman's health problems.

Liz could still remember her excitement when she received her credentials to Mrs. Roosevelt's correspondents association. She fondly recalled those early press conferences, when she and the other women reporters wore hats and white gloves and were served tea. A great deal in the world had changed since those days.

Mrs. Roosevelt died November 7, 1962, at the age of seventy-eight. Liz was grateful she had had the opportunity to see Mrs. Roosevelt during her visit to The Elms. Vice President and Mrs. Johnson attended the funeral, along with Presidents Truman, Eisenhower, and Kennedy.

The following year President Kennedy, Vice President Johnson, and their advisers decided to make a trip to Texas. They needed solid support in Texas if they were to carry out the administration's programs.

The trip appeared to be a great success. Cheering crowds turned out to greet the handsome young president and his glamorous wife, Jackie. Suddenly, shots rang out. President Kennedy was killed. And suddenly, Lyndon Johnson was president.

When President Johnson returned to Washington he asked Liz to stay on and "help Lady Bird all you can." The two women had been close friends for twenty years. Liz was eager to help in any way she could.

In early December, Liz visited with Mrs. Johnson at The Elms. She made suggestions for putting together a staff to help Mrs. Johnson handle her new duties as First Lady.

"As for me, Lady Bird — Mrs. Johnson," Liz caught herself a moment too late. She saw the slight change in her friend's expression. Liz realized Mrs. Johnson was no more pleased with this new formality than she was. Both women knew it was necessary. "As for me, Mrs. Johnson," Liz continued, "I'd like to be your press secretary."

"Why, of course, Liz. I'd love to have you as my press secretary. And my chief of staff as well," the First Lady said.

Remembering those early press conferences of Mrs. Roosevelt's, Liz already had some ideas of what to do — and what not to do. She gathered a group of newswomen and asked for their suggestions also.

Many people, Liz among them, saw similarities between Mrs. Johnson and Mrs. Roosevelt. Liz also saw marked differences.

Mrs. Roosevelt considered herself a journalist, although she had no formal training for the work. Mrs. Johnson had a degree in journalism from the University of Texas, but except for *The Daily Texan* she had never worked as a reporter. Both women were sensitive to the needs of the press.

Mrs. Roosevelt never hesitated to speak out on any subject about which she had strong feelings. She was not concerned about how her stand would reflect on her husband's administration. She didn't care that her actions on behalf of racial equality often hurt her popularity. She quickly became a political figure in her own right.

Mrs. Johnson had no desire for personal recognition. She was eager to do all she could to help her husband achieve his goals.

Both women had fought to overcome shyness and a reluctance to undertake public speaking. Both women shared traits of graciousness, courtesy, and loyalty.

Both had traveled extensively for their husbands. Mrs. Roosevelt acted as "the eyes and ears" for her husband. Travel was a grave physical hardship for Roosevelt. Mrs. Johnson visited the Job Corps, Head Start, and other War on Poverty programs around the nation so that she could report back to her busy husband. Her visits ranged from small family farms to sprawling national parks.

"I like to see the people behind the statistics," she told Liz. "It makes Lyndon's memos and working papers come alive for me."

The two presidents' wives had very different attitudes toward flying. Mrs. Roosevelt loved to fly, ever since her first flight with Amelia Earhart in 1933. On at least one occasion she took over the controls of a plane for a few moments.

Mrs. Johnson's fear of flying very nearly equaled Liz's own. She simply did a better job of hiding it.

"The Secret Service complains to me every time you and Lady Bird fly together," President Johnson told Liz. "Y'all just make each other worse."

The president had no qualms about flying. He had even used a helicopter, which he called the *Johnson City Windmill,* for his barnstorming 1948 campaign for United States senator from Texas.

In April 1964 Mrs. Johnson received an honorary degree from Texas Woman's University in Denton. Liz's great aunt, Birdie Robertson Johnson, helped establish the school in 1901.

Later that month Mrs. Johnson flew from Washington to Cleveland to address the Riverview Golden Age Center. The plane hit turbulence. Liz was afraid they wouldn't make it — to their destination or to their own "golden age."

Dr. Janet Travell, the first woman to serve as personal physician to a president, was on the plane. Ten women reporters and several Secret Service agents also were on the commercial airliner.

The tossing and lurching of the plane alarmed the passengers. Dr. Travell, working on her needlepoint, seemed the only calm person aboard.

Two lightning-like discharges of static electricity hit the plane. Liz leaped almost into Dr. Travell's lap. A Secret Service agent moved across the aisle to the seat next to Mrs. Johnson.

The plane landed safely. Mrs. Johnson kept her appointment at the senior citizens' home. She appeared much more composed than she could possibly have felt. She smiled, shook hands with everyone, and gave her speech as scheduled.

Liz ordered the Secret Service to arrange cars to drive the group back to Washington.

Later that year, Liz received a rather large, bulky package. She tore it open. There was the straw tote bag she had left on the press bus on the day of the assassination. Betty Harris, one of the women reporters who had been on the bus in Dallas, had returned it to her. Liz felt weak as the remembered horror of that awful day once again swept over her.

In addition to Liz, Mrs. Johnson's staff included her social secretary, Bess Abell, and her personal secretary, Ashton Gonella. Mrs. Johnson began keeping a diary of her life in the White House.

Liz's staff included Simone Poulaine, Marta Ross, Marcia Maddox, and two secretaries, Oghda O'Gulian and Lenora Haag.

Liz dressed carefully each morning before going to her offices in the East Wing of the White House. She never knew how long her work day would last or whom she would meet. She might talk to the White House dog handler, greet a tour busload of visitors, or be introduced to a visiting head of state.

President Johnson had been in office a year. He decided to campaign for the November 1964 elections.

"Lady Bird's going on a whistlestop trip," President Johnson told Liz. "Arrange it."

"Why, I think that's wonderful, Mr. President." Liz grinned up at him. "In fact, that's the best news I've had all day."

The tall president leaned forward, squinting his eyes somewhat as he often did. He studied her face carefully. Then he caught on to the reason for her enthusiastic good humor. A train trip meant she wouldn't have to fly. He chuckled and left her office as abruptly as he had entered.

The *Lady Bird Special* rolled 1,682 miles through the South, with almost fifty stops along the way. At each stop Mrs. Johnson appeared on the back platform of the train. She received greetings and usually flowers from the town's officials. Then she spoke a few words. Her soft, Southern accent carried the president's message to the people.

Mrs. Lindy Boggs was co-sponsor of the trip. She was the wife of Congressman Hale Boggs of Louisiana. Like Mrs. Johnson, Lindy was a daughter of the South. She was attractive and energetic, poised and gracious. Liz loved working with her. The two women became close friends.

President Johnson won the election. Hubert H. Humphrey of South Dakota was vice president.

Johnson felt very comfortable with the press — too comfortable for his own good, Liz often thought.

Once he picked up his beagles, Him and Her, by their ears. Photographs of the incident appeared in just about every newspaper and magazine. Another time he flipped his shirt up to show press photographers the scar from his recent operation.

Thousands of people phoned or wrote to the White House to protest what they believed was cruelty to animals and un-presidential conduct. Inevitably, Liz had to handle many of the protests.

Liz invited a group of friends and White House staff members to come to her home on Woodway Lane on Friday evening, March 29, 1968. The president's supporters were eager to begin work on the forthcoming election campaign.

Mrs. Johnson dropped by. Her dark eyes sparkled with enthusiasm as she asked questions or made suggestions. She was eager for President Johnson to have the opportunity to continue his Great Society programs. "There's so much work yet to be done," she said.

Sunday night Liz was in her pajamas, ready for bed. First she wanted to watch President Johnson's speech on television.

Johnson, appearing even more somber than usual, announced in detail a plan to halt the bombing in North Vietnam.

Then Liz saw him pause, moisten his lips, and take a deep breath. She recognized the signs of a speaker about to depart from his prepared text. She was partly right. The president had decided on which of two possible endings he would use.

"Accordingly," he said, "I will not seek, and I will not accept, the nomination of my party for another term as your president."

Liz was stunned. She grabbed the phone and asked the White House operator for Mrs. Johnson.

"Oh, Liz," Mrs. Johnson said. "You were so much on my mind. I knew you'd be so disappointed. But you mustn't forget how much we've done," she added in a gentle, reassuring voice.

The president's last-minute decision to resign at the end of his term caught all but a very few people by surprise. Even the small number who knew he was thinking of it hoped he would change his mind.

The days from April 1 to January 20 flew past. There was so much to be done. So many projects to complete. So much to clear out or pack away. As Inauguration Day neared, President Johnson's loyal White House staff worked frantically. That was the best way they knew to cope with their sadness.

In early October Liz made a speech for the United Press editors at a formal dinner. She barely made it through. She stepped down from the podium, almost doubled over in pain and burning with sudden fever. Les rushed her to Georgetown University Hospital. She had an emergency appendectomy that night.

When she woke up the next morning, she discovered Les, still dressed in his tuxedo, asleep on the floor beside her bed.

"He's been there all night," the nurse told her. "Now *that's* love!"

Her room quickly looked like a florist's shop. As soon as Liz recovered enough to sit up in bed, she demanded and got her portable typewriter. With a phone within reach and her typewriter on a lap tray, she kept up her work as best she could.

President Johnson sent his best wishes for a speedy recovery. He added a piece of personal advice: "Don't go showing your scar to just any old reporter, not even in confidence or off the record."

The night before Inauguration Day the Johnsons gave a farewell buffet supper for their staff.

The next day President Johnson — *former* President Johnson and the *former* First Lady, Liz had to remind herself — drove away from the White House. Liz saw Mrs. Johnson turn and wave goodbye to her.

Liz held up a big sign: "Culpepper thanks you, Mr. President!"

Les had bought a bottle of champagne. He knew Liz would need cheering.

"Well, here's to the Great Society," Liz toasted.

Les touched his glass to hers. "Here's to the girl from Salado," he replied.

13. A Second Life

When they got home, Liz rushed to her private phone.

"I want to call the White House just one more time," she said. She was too late. The special line from Woodway Lane to the White House had been disconnected.

Liz was disappointed but not surprised. What did surprise her was that several of the household appliances mysteriously didn't work. "That's what happens," she joked, "with Republicans in office."

The next morning Liz announced her determination to write a book about her experiences in the White House. She wanted to get all the details down on paper while they were still fresh in her mind.

"I'll probably be hard to live with for a few months," she warned her husband.

"So what else is new?" Les said, giving her a quick hug. He encouraged her to get started.

Liz went to her study upstairs. Her assistant, Cynthia Wilson, worked beside her.

She felt like a journalist again as she began banging away at a manual typewriter.

She had been trained to get the "five Ws" of any story: *who, when, what, where,* and *why*. As she worked, she often called on her colleagues in the Washington press corps and former White House staff members as well as the Johnsons themselves and their families and friends. They helped her remember names, dates, times, places, and quotes.

Liz chose *Ruffles and Flourishes* as the title of her book. Nothing reminded her of the might and majesty of the presidency more than those few bars of music for drum and full brass that traditionally precede the more familiar "Hail to the Chief."

Liz worked on the book from January through July 1969. Doubleday & Company published it in 1970.

The book was more successful than she had dared hope. It was a Book of the Month selection and appeared briefly on the *New York Times* best-seller list. Liz was invited to appear on talk shows. She received invitations to speak around the country.

Liz remained active in the Women's National Press Club. The club voted unanimously to admit men to membership in January 1971. Two days later the National Press Club, which had banned women for forty years, opened their membership. Esther Van Wagoner Tufty, Liz's old friend and mentor, was the first woman member.

Hill and Knowlton, an international public relations firm, invited Liz to join them as a vice president in February 1972.

Les and Liz continued to follow political news with intense interest.

June 17, 1972, was their twenty-eighth wedding anniversary. They were at their breakfast table, planning how to spend the day, when a story in the *Washington Post* caught Les's attention. They read it together in stunned disbelief.

During the presidential campaign, some men had been arrested. They were charged with breaking into the National Democratic Committee's headquarters in the Watergate Apartment building. The men admitted they were members of a committee to reelect President Nixon. In September, two former White House aides were among those indicted on charges of conspiracy in connection with the break-in.

President Nixon remained very popular with many voters. On November 8 he was elected to a second term by a large margin. He was inaugurated January 20, 1973.

Two days later, January 22, former president Lyndon Johnson died of a heart attack in Texas.

Liz was watching the "CBS Evening News." Walter Cronkite had received a phone call from Johnson's press aide, Tom Johnson. Cronkite relayed the news to his audience within moments.

Shocked, Liz rushed to phone Mrs. Johnson at the LBJ Ranch in Texas.

"Oh, yes, Liz, I would feel better if you could come," Mrs. Johnson said. "Thank you."

Liz flew to Texas the next day with Bess Abell.

Johnson's flag-draped casket was placed atop the grand staircase in the Great Hall of the LBJ Library and Museum in Austin. The body lay in state for a day.

Mrs. Johnson, Liz, and Bess Abell flew back to Washington, where the body lay in state in the Capitol Rotunda. The body was returned to Texas. Johnson was buried at Stonewall, just down the road from his ranch.

On the day of Johnson's death, another event took place that for the moment went almost unnoticed. Sarah Weddington, a young Austin lawyer, believed the United States Constitution protected the fundamental right of a woman to decide whether to have children. She had argued her case, *Roe v. Wade,* before the Supreme Court. On January 22, 1973, the Supreme Court's seven-to-two decision declared Texas' law prohibiting abortion was unconstitutional.

More Watergate stories had begun to appear in the *Washington Post.* Bob Woodward, a young police reporter, had been assigned to cover the Watergate break-in. He and another reporter, Carl Bernstein, continued to search for facts. They began to believe the trail led to the

White House. Their story won the Pulitzer Prize in 1973.

Spiro Agnew, President Nixon's vice president, faced charges unrelated to the Watergate break-in. He resigned from office October 12 that same year. President Nixon appointed Gerald Ford as the new vice president.

The Watergate scandal had grown bigger than anyone might have imagined.

"It's like a ridiculous sophomore prank," Liz told Les. "Imagine, grown men in face masks, tiptoeing around, trying to bug a political party!"

People throughout the country began to talk about impeaching President Nixon. In March 1974 a federal grand jury concluded President Nixon was a co-conspirator in the Watergate affair. A few weeks later, four top presidential aides resigned. President Nixon addressed the nation. He accepted responsibility for the affair, but he denied knowledge of it.

As much as he loved newspaper writing, Les began to wonder if he should continue. The journalism profession was changing in many ways. The almost instant coverage of breaking news that television provided was changing the public's expectations.

"Big newspapers have taken over, syndicating special series," Liz said. "The days of the 'mom and pop' news bureau like we had when we started out are over, Les." Liz urged Les to join her at Hill and Knowlton.

"I've been a newspaperman all my life," Les replied. "I don't know if I'd be any good at public relations."

"You'll be better than I am," Liz assured him. "You have more patience and you're better with people."

Les resigned his position as Washington correspondent for Newspapers, Inc. In June 1974 he joined Hill and Knowlton as a vice president. Liz insisted he be given the same rank and salary as hers. They were working together again.

On their thirtieth anniversary, June 17, Les wrote this note to Liz:

My dearest Liz,

The last thirty years would have been unbearable without you . . . I love you very much, very much, and I am so proud of your many accomplishments . . .

Liz had agreed to address a conference of the National Association of Legal Secretaries in Houston on Wednesday, July 24, 1974. A newspaperwoman to her very heart, Liz regretted having to leave Washington for even a short time. The Watergate scandal was so incredible, people seemed almost to be holding their breath.

"It's like following a James Bond plot," she said.

"Don't worry, honey," Les promised her. "I'll keep you posted on every new development."

"Les, you're the only person I know who follows the news more closely than I do," Liz told him.

Les drove Liz to the airport. They waited together until time for Liz to board her plane. They kissed goodbye.

Liz scarcely had time to check into her hotel room before Les phoned her. "The Supreme Court has ruled that Nixon has to turn over the Watergate tapes," he said.

He phoned several more times with quips she could include in her speech on the rapidly changing national news. He told her he missed her.

Liz's brother George and his wife, Jean, were living in Houston. Liz phoned their home to let them know she was in town. To her delight, Liz learned that her sister, Alice, was visiting George and Jean.

"Come on down to the hotel and spend the night with me," Liz urged her sister. "We can have a nice long visit after my speech tonight."

After the speech, Liz had far too much nervous energy to be sleepy. The two women kept up their animated conversation until late. Their favorite topic was their large family, with more than its share of colorful characters.

The phone rang.

"That's probably Les calling again," she said, laughing as she picked up the phone.

For a second Liz was pleased and surprised to recognize the voice of her son, Scott, calling from Austin. Then, with alarm, she caught the strained tone.

"Mom," Scott said, his voice breaking. "This is the hardest thing I've ever had to do. Dad died tonight of a heart attack." He added the few details he knew. "It was very sudden, Mom," he told her. "At least we know he didn't suffer."

Liz was shocked and disbelieving in the same moment. She grabbed a pencil and jotted down the plane reservations Scott had made for her.

How could Les be dead?

He was fifty-two, in good health as far as anyone knew. Liz tormented herself with guilt. Had she overlooked warning signs? Was there anything she could have done? How could she not have been there with him? How could she carry on without the close companionship they had shared for thirty years?

Even as these thoughts tore through her mind, she raced around the hotel room, stuffing clothes into her suitcase.

Alice had never recovered from the death of her husband, Judge John Romberg, in 1971. She tried to offer words of comfort. She knew there were none.

Scott had first called his Uncle George, looking for his mother. As soon as George received Scott's call, he hurried to the hotel. When his sisters finished packing, he drove them to the airport. Alice flew back to Washington with Liz.

Liz had tried to phone Christy, but the phone was off the hook. Liz phoned a neighbor and asked him to drive over. A sad and weeping Christy met her mother at the airport. With her were Congressman J. J. "Jake" Pickle and his wife, Beryl.

Ruth Baker, Liz's housekeeper for fifteen years, had readied everything at the Woodway Lane house. Liz and Les had shared the home for twenty-five years. Liz had expected life there to go on forever. From the moment she stepped in, she felt Les's absence achingly.

She had never imagined herself a widow.

One of the first persons to phone her to offer his condolences was Republican Senator John Tower of Texas.

Bella Abzug was next. She had been a Democratic congresswoman from New York. Liz knew her from the Women's Movement and the ERA fight. The deep, rich tones of Bella's voice reached out with comfort even more than the sympathetic words themselves.

Lindy Boggs came to the house. Les and Liz had waited with Lindy when word came that the plane carrying Congressman Hale Boggs of Louisiana was missing.

A memorial service was held for Les Saturday morning at St. Alban's Episcopal Church in Washington.

Les Carpenter was a widely known and respected Washington journalist. The church was packed with government officials and journalists. Many of them offered eulogies. Congressman Pickle praised Les as "one of the best reporters ever to work in Washington."

Liz and her family flew to Austin. After a service at St. David's Episcopal Church, Les was buried in Oakwood Cemetery. Les's father, John W. Carpenter, sat next to Liz. Like most parents, he had never expected his son to die before him.

Liz and the family returned to Scott's Austin home. Friends came by to offer condolences. Following the Southern custom, many brought food. Luci Baines Johnson sent a large roast.

Back in Washington, Liz searched for the strength to continue her life. They had always been a pair, she and her husband. Their many friends had pronounced "Les and Liz" almost as one word. Now she had to adjust to being alone instead of being part of a couple.

On August 9, 1974, President Nixon resigned rather than face impeachment. He was the first United States president ever to resign from office. The vice president, Gerald Ford, became president.

Liz was still too numb with shock and grief to follow the news as closely as she and Les would have together.

Liz realized she mustn't let herself sink into perpetual mourning. One day, as she visited with a dear friend, she admitted the problems she was having adjusting to Les's death.

Her friend, also a widow, talked to Liz firmly. "You can't go on this way," she said. "You must realize you've been given a chance at a second life. Make the most of it!"

A chance at a second life! Somehow the words put her loss in a different perspective.

She determined to remain active. She hurled her boundless energies back into the fight for the Equal Rights Amendment.

Liz kept busy writing, giving speeches, raising funds, and rallying supporters. She worked as hard as she could during the week. Still unwilling to submit to solitude, she spent weekends visiting her friends.

The proposed Twenty-seventh Amendment to the United States Constitution stated: "Equality under the law shall not be denied or abridged by the United States or any State on account of sex."

Alice Paul, a suffragist from the 1920s, was the author of the first equal rights amendment. She was now an elderly woman. She worked tirelessly to get the necessary two-thirds vote in Congress.

To become law, an amendment next must be ratified by three-fourths of the states' legislatures. The ERA had been sent to the states for ratification in 1972. Twenty-two states ratified the amendment that same year. Eight more followed in 1973. Only eight more states were needed.

Liz was working for ratification when the University of Texas notified her that she had been chosen to receive a Distinguished Alumna Award. She flew to Austin for the ceremony on October 24, 1975.

Liz was honored for her distinguished career as a Washington journalist, her position in the Johnson administration, her book, *Ruffles and Flourishes,* and her continued efforts for the ERA.

Liz was as proud of the university's award as she was of any recognition she had ever received.

The fight for ratification of the Equal Rights Amendment was not going well. Liz and the others continued to work hard to get those last states.

Some states held out strongly against ratification. And some of the states that had agreed to the amendment were now moving to rescind the earlier vote.

The new First Lady, Mrs. Betty Ford, was an outspoken supporter of the ERA. She felt so strongly about it that friends made an ERA flag for her automobile fender post.

Many women legislators worked in their home states to get needed votes for ratification. Entertainment personalities, including humor columnist Erma Bombeck, actress Carol Channing, and comedienne Lily Tomlin, joined the effort. Women of both political parties or with no party affiliation worked side by side.

ERAmerica was created early in 1976 to help rally nationwide support before the deadline for ratification. ERAmerica was an umbrella agency to coordinate the efforts of organizations and individuals.

Liz, a lifelong Democrat, and Elly Peterson, a Republican, were co-directors of the ERAmerica office in Washington. Liz made no secret of the fact that she welcomed Republican women to the fight for ERA.

"They're bright, intelligent, well-educated women," Liz said. "They have a great deal to contribute."

Liz and Elly were good friends in spite of their political differences.

"Oh, I believe in a two-party system," Liz teased her friend. "I just think the Democrats should be the ones in power."

Liz was delighted when Elly agreed to live in the Woodway Lane house. They shared household tasks. Whoever got home first started supper. Almost every evening the two held "mixers," or informal get-togethers, and planning sessions for ERA supporters.

The hard work, along with the companionship that now filled the empty house, began to ease Liz into an acceptance of widowhood.

14. Grass Roots

Finally, two years after Les's death, Liz believed the time was right to make a more lasting plan for the rest of her life.

She would return to her roots. She would go back to Texas.

"You'll do just fine for a year," Liz's daughter, Christy, predicted. "Then you'll regret leaving Washington."

Secretly, Liz suspected her daughter might be right.

Liz flew to Austin. She had lived there as a child, gone to school in Austin, and graduated from the University of Texas. Since moving to Washington, she had been back numerous times on business trips and for family visits. This time she looked at the city from a different perspective.

She realized that in such a short visit she couldn't choose the place that would be her home for the rest of her life. She turned the project over to her niece, Carol Sutherland Hatfield. Carol was Tommy's oldest daughter. Once again, Liz returned to Washington.

Carol searched for just the right house. She concentrated her efforts in the hills west of Austin. She knew her aunt wanted a view of the river and of the city. She wanted a home suited for entertaining. She wanted a guest house on the property.

"I've found the perfect place for you, Liz," Carol told her aunt on the phone on the Fourth of July. "It's your dream house. Only you'll have to come get it right away or someone else will snap it up."

Liz fell in love with the house as soon as she saw it. Rather, she fell in love with the possibilities. Built of yellow brick and native limestone, the house clung to the side of an oak-shaded hill. Liz could look down at the Colorado River. She could look across the river and see the Capitol dome and the University of Texas Tower.

She named the house "Grass Roots." The term had a double meaning for her. In one sense she was putting down her own roots in the soil of her home state. In another sense, she was playing on the term "grass roots politics," or politics on the local level.

Liz's many friends had a surprise for her when she returned to Washington. They arranged a gala farewell for her at the historic Ford's Theater. Mrs. Johnson and her daughters, Lynda and Luci, joined in the tribute. Pearl Bailey, Erma Bombeck, Carol Channing, Frances "Sissy" Farenthold, Mark Russell, and Gloria Steinem all took part.

Before the evening ended, Liz shed tears of sadness as well as tears of laughter. How could she bear to leave such wonderful friends and the glittering national capital she loved so dearly?

It was far too late to change her mind. She had sold the Woodway Lane house and bought her Hill Country house in Austin. She had sent her housekeeper, Ruth Baker, on ahead to get things ready.

Liz decided to return to Texas by way of a slow car trip through the South. She had come to know this part of the country through campaign whistlestops and Mrs. Johnson's visits as First Lady. She was eager to see what changes had taken place in the dozen years since President Lyndon Johnson's Civil Rights Act of 1964 and Mrs. Johnson's tour.

Her friend Betty Talmadge, spirited daughter of the South and former wife of Senator Herman Talmadge of Georgia, was the perfect companion. The two set off.

When they reached New Orleans they stayed with Lindy Boggs in her home in the French Quarter.

Liz and Lindy had worked on Senator George McGovern's presidential campaign. Liz and Les were with Lindy Boggs that awful night in October 1972 when the plane carrying Congressman Hale Boggs was lost in Alaska. The women waited together for words of his fate.

When Congressman Boggs' presumed death was declared, the people of Louisiana urged Lindy to take his place. She was elected to fill Louisiana's Second Congressional District seat. She was the first woman from Louisiana to be elected to a national office.

Now, four years later, the women came together again, sharing the common bonds of friendship and widowhood. Liz felt she drew courage from this slender, dark-haired woman's gentle strength.

Liz's niece, Karen Sutherland, had agreed to meet Liz at Congresswoman Boggs' home. Karen would drive Liz the rest of the way to her new home.

Karen was the daughter of George and Jean Sutherland, Liz's brother and sister-in-law. The previous summer, twenty-three-year-old Karen had stayed with Liz in Washington and worked as a tour guide at the Washington Monument. Every day she showed thousands of tourists the view from the top of the marble and granite structure that her Aunt Liz called "an exclamation mark against the sky of Washington."

Now Karen taught school in Spring Branch, near her family's home in Houston. She arranged to take off enough time to drive to New Orleans and back.

Karen thought surely Liz had given her the wrong directions. She checked the address, 623 Bourbon Street, and stared doubtfully at the plain gate in the wall. This couldn't be a private home. She opened the gate and stepped into a tranquil courtyard with a fountain, trailing bougainvillea, and delicate wrought-iron benches and balconies.

Karen found more surprises inside the house, built in 1795. The nineteenth-century furnishings, sparkling chandeliers, and canopied beds enchanted her. She enjoyed the unfamiliar seasonings of New Orleans food.

Most of all, she thrilled to the interesting conversation among the women. Liz, Lindy Boggs, and Betty Talmadge knew a great deal about national politics. Each woman had strong convictions.

"I think," Lindy Boggs said, peering over the tops of her half-glasses, "the White House is within the grasp of women." She believed a woman might someday be elected president.

"Well, that would be wonderful," Liz agreed. Dressed in one of her colorful, flowing caftans, Liz set aside her coffee cup. Leaning forward to make her point, she added, "We all know that's not the way it works. Before we can have a woman president in this country, we're going to have to elect more women governors and women senators. We need to see more women involved in politics at every level, from grass roots all the way to Washington."

Karen stayed in the Boggs home overnight. The next morning Betty Talmadge returned to her home in Georgia. Liz and Karen loaded up Karen's car and started out.

Karen was still feeling the excitement of the night before.

"Aunt Liz, how do you make so many wonderful friends?" Karen asked as she drove.

"Parties," Liz replied without a moment's hesitation. "I give a lot of parties. I invite interesting people. We get together to enjoy good food and, above all, good conversation."

Karen tucked away this piece of advice. She would have to try that sometime.

As the women drove across the Sabine River and entered Texas, Liz could imagine she once again heard her mother's voice, urging her to "Remember who you are."

Karen enjoyed hearing about her grandmother, Mary E, whom she never knew. She laughed appreciatively as Liz told her some of the childhood exploits of her father, George.

Liz could turn the simplest incident into an outrageously funny story. She entertained Karen with tales of their Sutherland and Robertson ancestors who had crossed the South from Alabama and Tennessee to settle in Texas nearly a century and a half ago.

Liz was coming home, in spirit as well as in fact.

Ruth Baker, Liz's housekeeper, met her at the door. "Just three weeks ago we were in Washington packing all this stuff," Ruth said. "Now here we are unpacking it in your new home. It all fits just fine." Ruth had a gift for saying just the right thing to comfort folks.

The aroma of Ruth's special pot roast soon filled the house. Even the cold driving rain that hampered the unloading of the moving van couldn't dampen Liz's spirits now.

Liz plunged into the task of remodeling her new home.

She tore out walls to make more open space, enclosed the front porch to create a breakfast room with a cathedral-style ceiling, and converted the garage into a living room with a bay window and fireplace.

The remodeling was finally complete. Sue Brandt McBee, a former classmate of Liz's at the University of Texas who had become a writer, visited Grass Roots. She described Liz's new home in an article for *Austin Homes and Gardens.*

Liz had a Jacuzzi built in the form of a stone wishing well. The bubbling water was Liz's favorite way to relax or to entertain.

"It's big enough for eight friends or six enemies," she told Christy one day over the phone. Christy often teased her mother, calling the Jacuzzi "Mother's favorite decadence."

Liz still had to earn a living. She worked as a consultant for the LBJ Foundation, which helps raise funds to support the Lyndon Baines Johnson Presidential Library and Museum in Austin. She continued to accept invitations to speak to national conference groups. She wrote a series of columns for the *Austin American-Statesman,* syndicated through the *Dallas Times Herald.*

Liz taught a course in journalism for the School of Communications at the University of Texas. Inspired by the example of Bob Woodward and Carl Bernstein of Watergate fame, many students had chosen careers as investigative reporters. They were eager to hear everything Liz could tell them about covering the political beat.

"I have to warn you," Liz told the class, "I got my degree back in 1942 B.C. That's 'Before Communications.' In those days we just called it journalism."

The "Forty Acres," as the university campus was called, was not so crowded in those days. Students and teachers knew each other, and not just in the classroom.

She told them about one of her favorite professors, DeWitt C. Reddick. "Professor Reddick was more than just my journalism teacher," Liz said. "He was my friend. He and Mrs. Reddick came to Washington for my wedding in 1944."

She described the old Journalism Building with its *Texas Ranger* and its *Daily Texan* offices, where she and Les Carpenter had both worked. "The *Texan* office was a big, bare room with a horseshoe-shaped table — the 'slot' as we called it. Editors and headline writers and reporters wrote on upright manual typewriters. It's still hard for me to compose on anything but a battered old typewriter with a worn out ribbon and two stuck keys.

"We all dreamed of roaming the world and writing prize-winning stories. Back then journalism was more a state of mind than an academic subject," she explained.

Liz also taught a class in essay writing. As much as she enjoyed working with the bright young students, she did not believe she was cut out to be a teacher.

"I've made a horrible mistake," she admitted on the second day of class. "I told you everything I know the first day."

When the semester ended, the class took Liz to Scholz Garten for lunch. They presented their teacher with an apple in the form of a wooden salad bowl.

Liz began writing a book, *Hail to the Comic Relief,* a collection of presidential and political humor. She set up an office in the guest house.

Liz and her assistant, Shirley James, worked at two desks, with two phones, facing the sliding glass doors with a distractingly beautiful view of Austin. Behind the women a fire crackled in the stone fireplace.

"Now, isn't this cozy?" Liz asked, banging away contentedly on a battered old upright manual typewriter.

"You may be cozy," Shirley retorted. "I'm freezing!"

Shirley looked forward to noontime. She could go into the house, get warm, and thaw her frozen fingers while she ate the delicious lunches Ruth Baker prepared for them.

Inside the main house Ruth Baker imposed her own order on things. Domestic chores had never been high on Liz's list of favorite activities.

Although Liz had lived in the country as a small child, she had lived in the nation's very metropolitan capital for more than thirty years. She had no idea how to cope with septic tanks that turned stubborn after heavy rains, snakes that sunned themselves on the warm rocks of her Jacuzzi, and deer that adored munching on her geraniums.

Liz's neighbors included Henrietta and Jens Jacobsen, both administrators at the University of Texas. Henrietta was a former mayor of West Lake and continued to serve on the Zoning and Planning Commission. She did all she could to help Liz settle into her new home. Liz had only to pick up the phone and Henrietta rushed down the hill, armed with screwdriver, hoe, or other rescue tools.

Liz lost little time in starting to give one of her fabulous parties. Parts of the house were gutted with remodeling still going on — but there was a perfectly good lawn, wasn't there?

During the party a sudden Hill Country storm swept across the river.

"Quick, everyone! Into the house," Liz directed.

The guests scampered into the house. In the unfinished living room they threw planks on sawhorses for improvised tables and continued the party.

Once again, Liz's formula of good food and good conversation saved the day.

Liz continued to accept speaking engagements. In February 1979 she was in Houston taking part in a roast for her good friend Maxine Mesinger, columnist for the *Houston Chronicle*. When she returned to her hotel room she discovered her jewelry had been stolen. Seven of the pieces had been given to her by Les during their marriage.

When she had had more time to settle in at Grass Roots, Liz gave a dinner party in honor of her cousin, Malcolm McLean. Malcolm had lived near the Sutherlands in Belton. He had been one of the many students who had stayed in Mary E's home at 1611 West Avenue while attending the university. Malcolm and Liz's brother Tommy had grown up as close friends. Malcolm was now a professor at the University of Texas at Arlington. He had just finished the fifth volume of his history of the Robertson Colony in Texas.

Liz asked her guests to "dress Texan." Malcolm came as the original *empresario,* Sterling Clack Robertson.

Liz chose a menu of the same ingredients her ancestors would have used. She built the meal around venison, beans, corn, rice, and pecans. In the kitchen of Grass Roots, Tommy stood by to insure that Liz prepared the foods with as much authenticity as possible.

When it came time to eat, however, Tommy skipped the "Old Nashville cornbread."

"I ate enough cornbread as a child to last me all my life," he insisted.

Here at Grass Roots, surrounded by so many of her Texan relatives and her many friends, Liz asked herself why it had taken her two years to decide to come home.

15. Madam Secretary

Liz Carpenter did what millions of other Americans did on Thursday, January 20, 1977. She watched the inauguration on television.

Liz had worked in the campaign to help elect Jimmy Carter. She was delighted to have a Democrat back in the White House.

She watched the new president as he took the oath of office as the thirty-ninth president. She heard his address as he urged the people to have "fresh faith in an old dream."

She cheered when President Carter and his wife, Rosalyn, walked along Pennsylvania Avenue toward their new home in the White House. Their nine-year-old daughter, Amy, holding her parents' hands, skipped along between them. They were followed by other members of the Carter family.

The day was sunny and clear in the capital, but Liz could see snow on the ground. She could tell, from the way flags and banners and scarves and coattails were whipping around, that a strong wind was blowing. Liz knew only too well how cutting that wind could be. The weather on inauguration day was often the cruelest the capital city had to offer.

She was glad to be snug at home in Texas.

She sat in her favorite chair in her colorful living room. A small fire in the fireplace added warmth and a hearty glow. When she glanced away from the TV screen, she could see deer coming down the hill to graze their lazy way past her bay window.

She had invited friends to drop by Grass Roots for an informal celebration. Throughout the day they followed the ceremonies and festivities that accompany a presidential inauguration.

"You're going to miss it," her friends had warned. "You're going to wish you were there."

Always in the past she had been there. But she always had an important role to play — as a member of the Washington press corps or as a part of President Johnson's official staff. She didn't believe she would enjoy being an outsider, an onlooker.

"I received an invitation," Liz assured her concerned friends. "I could fly to Washington if I wanted to. Believe me," she added with a chuckle, "it's not as glamorous as it appears on television. It's more of an endurance test than anything. The crush of people — well, you just get trampled. The inaugural balls are so crowded you can't dance."

Liz was "a political animal," she admitted. She continued to follow the news from Washington with great interest. She wanted to see the nation heal the wounds of Watergate and move forward.

President Carter had planned his campaign thoroughly. One of the goals he wanted to achieve as president was a separate Department of Education.

Education was part of the Department of Health, Education, and Welfare, or HEW. The HEW had been established in 1953, during the administration of President Dwight D. Eisenhower.

Mrs. Oveta Culp Hobby, from Texas, had been the director of the Women's Army Corps (WAC) during World

War II. She was appointed as the first secretary of the department. She was the second woman ever to be named to cabinet rank.

President Carter named Shirley Mount Hufstedler as the secretary of education on October 30, 1979. She was sworn in December 6, 1979. Mrs. Hufstedler was a former judge of the U.S. Court of Appeals for the Ninth Circuit. She had been named to the federal court in 1968 by Lyndon Johnson. Many believed she was certain to be picked for the next U.S. Supreme Court vacancy.

Liz knew Shirley Hufstedler, although not well. The two had worked together in the Women's Movement. Liz had always worked to see more women in policy-making government positions. She was glad President Carter seemed to be honoring his promise to appoint women.

One day, sitting in the soothing, bubbling water of her heated Jacuzzi, Liz reviewed with satisfaction her accomplishments of the last years. The knife's edge of grief over Les's death had dulled. She was left with her many happy memories. She had made a good life for herself in Texas — active and full of purpose.

What ever made me think I'd miss Washington? she thought. *I don't ever plan to go back.*

A few days later, the phone rang. Shirley Hufstedler said, "Liz, you've got to come to Washington."

"Well, I don't know, Shirley," Liz said. "Before I left the White House in 1969 I cleaned out my office. I tried to sweep all my mistakes under the rug, but there wasn't room," she added, unable to resist a joke.

"I'm serious, Liz. I need you. Your country needs you. I want you to be part of the transition team for the Department of Education."

"You're going to accept, aren't you?" Tommy Sutherland asked.

Liz had called her brother to come and talk about Shirley Hufstedler's summons. They sat at the table in Liz's breakfast room, enjoying coffee and cinnamon rolls. Winter sunshine and pots of pink and red geraniums brightened the room.

"I have no desire to go back to Washington," Liz said. "How many times have I said that?"

Tommy gave his sister a disbelieving smile. The two were close friends and had always confided in each other. Tommy wasn't fooled by her denial.

"Well, it *is* nice to feel needed again," Liz admitted. "I have to say I haven't felt such persuasion since Lyndon Johnson used to pick me up by the ears."

That brought a hearty laugh from Tommy. He remembered the uproar caused by photographs of President Johnson lifting the White House beagles by their ears. Liz, as Mrs. Johnson's press secretary, had to explain that the president was not abusing the animals.

"It doesn't really hurt the dogs," she had told reporters. "I know, because sometimes the president picks *me* up by my ears! And I spend a lot of time in the doghouse."

Liz continued, talking herself into acceptance. "Our families have always believed in education. The reason Mother moved to Austin was so we could all have a university education. And anyway," she added, her decision made, "who am I to say 'no' to a cabinet secretary?"

President Carter formally nominated Liz as assistant secretary of education for public affairs in late January 1980.

Liz asked her assistant, Shirley James, to come with her. She found friends to take care of her Grass Roots home. She phoned her good friends, Douglass and Libby Cater, and arranged to stay with them in their Washington home. She packed seven suitcases and was on her way.

The first thing Liz did in Washington was the same task she had set for herself when she had come to the nation's capital in 1942. She went from office to office, paying her courtesy calls on official Washington. But there was a big difference this time. Then she had been as green as a sapling willow along Salado Creek. Now she was a knowledgeable Washington insider.

Most of the people she called on were old friends and former colleagues. Some were new friends from her work in the ERA effort and the Carter campaign.

Sarah Weddington was among the women working in the Carter administration. Sarah, who had argued the winning side in *Roe v. Wade* before the U.S. Supreme Court, had served three terms in the Texas House of Representatives. Jimmy Carter asked Sarah to lead White House efforts for an extension of time for ratification of the ERA and to implement other programs to promote equal treatment of women. When Liz returned to Washington, Sarah was assistant to the president.

Liz surprised herself by how much at home she felt as she returned to familiar surroundings.

"But my roots are in Texas now," she told Shirley Hufstedler. "I'll stay one year and do the job. Then it's back to Grass Roots for me."

Liz walked into her spacious corner office and eyed the contraption on her desk with suspicion.

"What's *that* ?" she demanded, pointing at the shiny new electric typewriter. "You know I can't work on that."

Within a few days her assistant, Shirley James, plunked down a battered old upright manual typewriter.

"Now that's more like it!" Liz exclaimed.

"I certainly hope so," Shirley said. "I had to scour the bowels of Washington to find it for you."

The Carter administration was eager to avoid any scandals such as those that had touched previous administrations. Liz had to fill out pages and pages of questions about her personal life, her family, her education, and her previous jobs.

One of the questions asked: "Do you have any relatives who might embarrass the president?" Liz thought for only a moment. Chuckling, she wrote firmly in the space provided for an answer, "THOUSANDS!"

Although she had been nominated by the president of the United States, the nomination had to be approved by the Senate. February 14 was the date set for the Senate confirmation hearing. Liz picked out her reddest red dress to wear for the occasion.

"I hope you'll all be my Valentine today," she told the senators.

Liz knew the importance of a good appearance. She thought a little color would be a good thing for Shirley Hufstedler too. After eighteen years as a judge, Secretary Hufstedler felt more comfortable in somber blacks, grays, and browns.

"You've been wearing judge's robes too long," Liz told her friend. "You need something brighter when you appear before the public or the press."

Liz's assistant, Shirley James, was about the same size as Shirley Hufstedler. Liz sent Shirley James shopping for new clothes for the secretary of education.

"I know what 'transition' in 'transition team' means," Shirley James told her co-workers. "It means you never finish your work and get to go home."

When time came for Liz to be sworn in, she held her infant grandson, Les Carpenter, in her arms as she repeated the oath.

"There's some doubt as to which one of us was actually sworn in as assistant secretary," she joked to newspaper reporters.

Liz lived with the Caters, and Shirley James had a small apartment. When Liz's friend from the Johnson administration, Simone Poulaine, came to Washington, Liz was reminded of her early Washington days in the Bedside Manor.

"Let's all share an apartment," she suggested.

Nothing came of the idea. Liz found her stay with the Caters exactly suited her.

Doug and Libby, both Southerners, extended gracious hospitality. Libby had been an active worker for women's rights. She and Liz had worked together many times. Doug Cater had been a White House special assistant to President Johnson.

As a young man, President Johnson had been a schoolteacher in South Texas. As president he often said, "Education is the only valid passport out of poverty."

Doug Cater had played an important role in shaping the education bills for the Johnson administration. Liz valued his knowledge and experience.

"I need to pick your brain," Liz often told him.

"I knew the president's ideas," Doug told Liz during one of their many evening chats. "I just tried to keep things going."

The year Liz promised to stay in Washington had passed quickly. In many ways it had been an exciting and fulfilling time. Unfortunately, the year ended on a frustrating and discouraging note.

For various reasons President Carter began to lose popularity. Many people believed he had not been able to carry out his foreign and domestic programs. Some women felt he had not kept his promise to appoint a fair proportion of women to his administration.

Even members of his own party began to doubt that he could be elected for a second term. Nevertheless, President Carter received the nomination at the Democratic National Convention.

The Republican candidate, Ronald Reagan, won the election on November 4, 1980, by a large margin. Reagan was sworn in as the fortieth president on Tuesday, January 20, 1981.

During his campaign, Reagan had vowed he would discontinue the new Department of Education. Liz was afraid he would keep his word. The hard work Shirley Hufstedler, Liz, and all the others had done would be destroyed.

Saddened, Liz left Washington to return to Austin on Sunday, January 25.

It was a joyous homecoming. Her family and her many Texas friends greeted her as she got off the plane at Robert Mueller airport. They rolled out the traditional red carpet for her. Austin's mayor, Carole McClellan, met Liz at the gate with a dozen yellow roses.

Inside the airport people waved banners and signs of welcome. One of the signs read, "Live and Let Liz."

"Let Liz what?" she asked with a mischievous grin.

The hectic pace Liz had kept up in Washington left her unable to settle down for long. Within a few days she was off again, beginning a series of speaking engagements across the country.

16. *Ann in the Mansion*

Liz enjoyed going to parties almost as much as she loved giving them. One memorable get-together was an informal evening with John Henry Faulk at his West Lake Hills home. His wife was busy with the couple's young son, John Henry Roman Numeral Three, as the elder Faulk called him.

Faulk had won his fight to clear his name of the false charges of the 1950s. He had moved back to Texas with his English-born second wife, Liz Peake Faulk.

Liz and John Henry, friends since childhood, were talking politics.

"I believe you need a sense of purpose and a sense of humor to survive in politics," Liz said.

"Well, Liz, darlin', you've got it backwards as usual," John Henry replied in his familiar drawl. "To survive in Texas politics your sense of humor's got to come first. I think about the only way you can tolerate Texas politics is with a sense of humor." Faulk mimed a look of horror. "Why, what if you took 'em seriously?"

An attractive woman, one of the Faulks' new neighbors, was among the guests that evening. She laughed as loudly as anyone at John Henry's wit. Liz turned to her.

"And what do you do?" Liz asked, starting the ritual of social conversation.

"I'm Ann Richards," the woman replied. "And I guess you could say I'm in Texas politics."

Liz was full of questions. Ann quickly told her story.

"Sarah Weddington — you know her? — she asked me to be her campaign manager. Well, she won. She's in her second term now. I'm her legislative assistant."

"Why, I think that's wonderful!" Liz exclaimed. "That's just what I'm always telling women to do. Get involved. Volunteer. Help raise money. That's how we'll get more women into elective offices.

"And yes, I know Sarah from the Texas Women's Political Caucus," Liz added. "I remember that beautiful long, reddish-blonde hair. She was still a law student at the University of Texas then."

In her Central Texas accent, not unlike Liz's own, Ann quickly filled in the details. While living in Dallas she had become known for her volunteer work and fund-raising skills. When she moved to Austin, she got a call, asking her to help Sarah Weddington campaign for the Texas House of Representatives. In 1972, Sarah was elected — the first woman elected to the House from Travis County.

Ann Richards also managed the successful campaign of Wilhelmina Delco. In 1974 Wilhelmina Delco became the first black woman in the Texas House of Representatives.

During Sarah's second term she asked Ann to be her legislative assistant. Ann represented Sarah on the Austin Transportation Study.

As Ann's political skills and confidence grew, she decided it was time to seek an elected office herself. In 1976 she won the Third Precinct seat on the Travis County Commissioners Court.

That was the same year that Liz returned to Austin to make Grass Roots her home. She had made a number of other changes in her life as she continued to adjust to widowhood. One of those changes was a return to the church of her childhood.

Les had been Episcopalian. When they married, Les had wanted them to attend church as a family.

"I don't mind," Liz assured him. "After all, Episcopalians are just Neiman-Marcus Methodists anyway." Liz found the liturgy and elaborate ceremony both beautiful and inspirational.

Now that she was home in Texas, she longed for the comfort of the familiar old hymns and the simple worship service of the church in which she had grown up, the University United Methodist Church.

She found that her writing and speeches had changed as well. She still drew on her experiences in Washington, and had an almost inexhaustible supply of political anecdotes. She had become more introspective as she searched for answers to questions she had never worried much about.

Many of her speeches and magazine articles contained advice on growing older with grace and humor. She got a lot of letters and phone calls from people asking for help dealing with the grief of losing a husband or wife. She didn't hesitate to put her advice into action.

Henrietta Jacobsen's husband, Jens, died in November 1983. One evening in early December, Liz went to her friend Henrietta's home.

"I've come to take you to supper at George and Jean Sutherlands' home," she said. "You'll like them."

"Oh, no, Liz. Thank you, but I can't," Henrietta said. "It's much too soon."

"You're coming. I'm staying right here until you do," Liz announced firmly. She sat down.

Henrietta offered her uninvited guest a glass of wine. Uncomfortably, she tried to make conversation. Finally she said, "All right, I can see you're not going to leave me alone. I give up. I'll go with you."

It was tough therapy, but Liz knew it was the best thing for her friend. She kept it up until she was sure Henrietta could deal with her grief.

When Liz's article, "Silver Lining," appeared in *Texas Monthly* magazine, syndicated columnist Erma Bombeck and others urged Liz to write another book. This one, they said, should talk about starting over after loss.

September 1, 1985, on her sixty-fifth ("Medicare") birthday, Liz started to work. This time she found the courage to switch from a typewriter to a word processor. Sitting in her home office, where she could look out at her geraniums, the grazing deer, and the Capitol and University Tower beyond, Liz began writing.

Once again Liz called on Shirley James for help. Liz had daily phone conversations with her brother Tommy. She asked her other relatives for help in recalling family events and supplying photographs and letters. She revived her childhood memories with the help of Sue Kone Drake. She talked to many of her friends from the university and from her early days at the *Austin American-Statesman.*

She went through her address book, phoning friends around the country, getting their advice on how they had turned personal grief into personal growth.

The book, *Getting Better All the Time,* was published by Simon and Schuster in 1987.

Liz's friends Coleen and Dick Hardin invited some people to come to their ranch near Lampasas for a weekend. Guests included Liz, Henrietta, Ray Daum, Lael and George Seagert, and Alma Jean and Fred Ward. The theme was "Teahouse of the August Moon."

In the evening the guests sat outside and enjoyed the full moon. Coleen and Dick encouraged them to listen for coyotes.

"Let's see if we can call 'em up," someone suggested.

They began slowly, timidly, at first. Soon their enthusiastic howling would have alarmed a pack of hungry wolves.

Howling at the full moon made them all feel great. They decided to get together once a month to repeat the experience. The Bay at the Moon Club was born. There were no elected officers, no bylaws, no dues. The only requirement was that each person must bring a book to share with the others or a poem to read or a song to sing.

The singing became a favorite aspect of the lunar celebrations. Soon the group was writing or adapting their own songs. They even began adding a bit of choreography.

"We're louder than we are good," one member admitted ruefully.

"Well, I think you're great," Liz said. "In fact, I think I should take y'all with me on my book promotion tour."

The group traveled through East Texas, performing and introducing Liz's *Getting Better All the Time*. Abbreviating the title, they soon became known as the GBATTS (pronounced GEE-BATS).

As their confidence grew, so did their repertoire. They were invited to entertain at senior citizens' centers, retirement homes, and charitable fundraisers. The number of performers varied. Martha Deatherage, a member of the university's music faculty, brought her talent to the group. Christian Smith joined the GBATTS. Cactus Pryor, television and radio personality, often acted as master of ceremonies.

Liz continued to watch Ann Richards' career develop. She was reelected to her seat on the Travis County Commissioners Court in 1980. In 1982 she announced her candidacy for state treasurer and won. She won reelection in 1986.

Liz learned that Ann and Henrietta had served together from time to time on the Zoning and Planning Commission. Liz also learned that she and Ann shared the same birthday: September 1.

"Liz, the speech is coming along just fine," Ann said on the phone one day.

She didn't have to say which speech. All of Ann's friends and political supporters knew she had been selected to give the Keynote Address at the Democratic National Convention in Atlanta in July 1988.

Ann's close advisers, Jane Hickie, Mary Beth Rogers, and Cathy Bonner, had all contributed to the draft of the speech. Professional political writers helped put the remarks in finished form.

"What I need from you, Liz," Ann continued, "are some good one-liners. We're gonna have some fun with this speech. We're gonna tell 'em how the cow ate the cabbage."

Ann Richards took her place at the podium. Her dress was an aqua shade of her favorite color, blue. Her white hair was piled high in a style that has become her trademark.

"After listening to George Bush all these years," she began, "I figured you needed to know what a *real* Texas accent sounds like." She continued in the same way, using humor and wit to make her points. She had to pause several times because the audience kept interrupting with laughter and applause.

The Keynote Address won a lot of national publicity for Ann Richards. When she returned to Austin, she called her close advisers together. She was thinking of running for governor.

Ann had started in politics as a fundraiser. She knew that money was essential to conduct a statewide campaign. She wouldn't undertake a campaign if she couldn't afford to see it through.

Ann Richards announced her candidacy on Saturday, June 10, 1989, on the south steps of the Capitol. Her parents, Cecil and Iona Willis, and her four children were at her side. The Waco High School band from Ann's hometown played.

Ann Richards was off to a great start.

As soon as Liz heard of Ann's candidacy, she was eager to help. Liz had worked in the campaign of Minnie Fisher ("Minnie Fish") Cunningham in the 1940s. She had campaigned for Frances ("Sissy") Farenthold in the 1970s.

The time was ripe. Liz could feel it. Texas was again ready to elect a woman governor. She outlined for Ann one of her favorite strategies: whistlestop campaigning. She even offered the services of the GBATTS.

The members excitedly planned new costumes and wrote new songs for the occasion. Henrietta bought an electronic keyboard. Liz coordinated their visits with local Democrats. They decorated a bus with campaign banners and toured East Texas, making stops at Corsicana, Palestine, Longview, and Tyler.

Ann Richards won the November 1990 election after a tough and hard-fought campaign. Texans all over the state celebrated her inauguration January 15, 1991. The grandest celebrations, of course, were in Austin.

Ann Richards took the oath of office with her hand on the Sam Houston Bible. She became the forty-fifth governor of Texas and the second woman governor of the state.

The winter day was crisp and clear, but a strong wind played havoc with banners and flags and hats and tents.

Liz and the GBATT performers, dressed in new red, white, and blue Western costumes, took their places on a high, wooden platform. The structure swayed in the nearly gale-force winds. The wind almost seemed to snatch the words of their song, *Richards!,* from their mouths. But nothing could disguise or diminish their jubilation.

Thousands of Texans lined Congress Avenue to watch the parades. Five of Tommy Sutherland's daughters, Carol Hatfield, Beth Weber, and Barbara, Kay, and Lin Sutherland, linked arms and marched along in a parade of their own. Sixth-generation Texans and strong supporters of the Women's Movement, they had cause to celebrate.

Even before the echo of the twenty-one-gun salute faded, a rumor made the rounds. The Queen of England had announced a visit to the United States. She might even come to Texas!

The Southwest Conference on Aging determined to have Erma Bombeck as their speaker for their meeting in San Antonio. For months the program planners had written and phoned Liz, begging her to urge Erma to accept the invitation.

Liz's entreaties may have persuaded Erma. She agreed, and Liz went to San Antonio to be with her friend from the ERA fight.

Ann Richards invited Erma and Liz to spend a night in the Governor's Mansion when they returned to Austin after the conference. Coleen and Dick Hardin had a supper party for them before they met at the Mansion.

Ann, Erma, and Liz, three good friends, talked and laughed late into the night. They had breakfast together the next morning. Liz packed up for her return to Grass Roots. Erma wanted a chance to visit in Liz's home and accepted a ride with her. Pressed for time, she reluctantly left her things tossed about the Sam Houston bedroom in the Mansion.

Time passed all too quickly. Erma had to return to the Mansion, pack, and rush to the airport. Liz's assistant offered to drive Erma back to the Mansion.

As they neared the Governor's Mansion, Liz's assistant said, "I'm afraid we'll have to detour around the block. Just look at all those tour buses parked there."

"Oh, God!" Erma exclaimed. "Don't let them be touring the bedrooms!"

The Queen of England was indeed coming to Texas!

Queen Elizabeth II scheduled trips to Austin, San Antonio, Dallas, and Houston. Governor Richards was the Queen's official hostess for her visit to Austin and the Capitol. LaVada Jackson of the governor's staff coordinated the affair.

Thousands of Texans, eager for a glimpse of royalty, gathered on May 20, 1991, to hear the Queen's address from the south steps of the Capitol. Her remarks set them cheering.

"No state commands such fierce pride and loyalty," she told her listeners. "Lesser mortals are pitied for their misfortune in not being born Texan."

Liz, with her Scot and English heritage dating back centuries, was as excited as anyone.

An elaborate supper and a reception were to be held at the Lyndon Baines Johnson Library. Liz ripped excitedly into the heavy, cream-colored formal invitation.

Governor Ann Richards and the former First Lady,

Lady Bird Johnson, were in the receiving line with Elizabeth II and Prince Philip. The Queen's gown was royal blue silk chiffon. She wore a diamond and sapphire necklace. Governor Richards chose her favorite shade of aqua. Mrs. Johnson wore pink with white beaded sleeves. Liz's dress was red with gold thread embroidery.

Liz learned that each person who passed through the receiving line had only a few seconds to say something to Her Majesty.

What could she say? Could she mention her British ancestress, the Countess of Sutherland? Could she tell how her forebears had come to America in the Colonial days? Should she say she had met the Queen Mother in Washington?

The line moved rapidly. Liz still had not decided. There she was, reaching out to clasp the white-gloved hand of the reigning British monarch.

Suddenly, the words came to her. "Thank you," she surprised herself by saying to the Queen of England, "for the British poets."

17. Calling All Women

Cathy Bonner, Jane Hickie, and Ann Richards had come up with an idea several years earlier.

"Wouldn't it be great," Jane said, "if we could get a Chair for Liz?"

In honor of the University of Texas's Centennial Year, 1983, the Board of Regents had endorsed an endowment plan. University funds would be used to match private gifts.

Liz's friends knew Liz loved the university. She was proud of being a distinguished alumna. She often spoke of the obligation to "give something back" for the education and opportunities one received. They decided to raise funds to endow a lectureship in Liz's honor.

Liz's former assistant, Shirley James, had completed her job as special events planner at Southwest Texas State University in San Marcos. She was chosen to be executive director of the effort to raise funds. Shirley was determined to keep the project a secret from Liz. She knew that Liz didn't make secret-keeping easy.

"Well, Shirley, I'm worried about you," Liz said each

time she saw her friend. "Have you found another job yet? Won't you let me do something to help you?"

"No, Liz," Shirley assured her. "I'm just not ready yet."

One day when they met, Liz didn't say a word about helping Shirley find a job. Instead she grinned, with a mischievous sparkle in her eyes, and talked about other things.

Uh-oh, Shirley thought. *Liz knows!*

Shirley set up an office in donated space in the United Bank. Dozens of Liz's friends agreed to serve on the committee. Mrs. Johnson was honorary chairperson. They sent out letters requesting donations.

The donations poured in. But something bigger was needed. If only they could get some really big-name stars to come to Austin. That would be a cinch to raise the needed money. If they could fill the Paramount Theater — but that was probably too much to hope.

"Watch me," Shirley said.

When Shirley contacted Liz's celebrity friends, they were delighted with the idea.

"A Celestial Evening . . . A Gala Honoring Liz Carpenter" was held at the Paramount Theater, July 7, 1983. Gray Hawn designed the sets. Barbara Vacker was in charge of catering services and accommodations for the stars.

Erma Bombeck and John Henry Faulk would be a part of the evening. So would Nancy Dickerson, well-known newswoman and colleague, and Marijane Maracle, Liz's friend and Alpha Phi sorority sister who had been Carol Channing's understudy in *Hello Dolly.* Congressman Jake Pickle played his harmonica, his usual contribution to a musical evening. Cactus Pryor, humorist and friend from the Sutherlands' early years in Austin, was master of ceremonies. Ann Richards, then state treasurer, was there. Mark Russell, popular political satirist from Washington, D.C., put on his act.

Dozens of Liz's friends "roasted and toasted" her

with their memories of her influence on their lives.

Liz's family came. Christy was there. Scott and his wife, Jean, and their young son, Les, flew in from Seattle. Five-year-old Les, dressed in a tuxedo, presented Liz a bouquet of roses.

The Celestial Evening performance and the dinner afterward raised more than $8,000 for the Liz Sutherland Carpenter Distinguished Lectureship series at the university.

"We wanted to get a Chair for you, Liz," Shirley told her. "At least we earned enough to get you a footstool." Shirley gave Liz a symbolic footstool for Grass Roots.

The first lecture was set for February 1985. When the time came to select the speaker, Liz had already made her choice: Madam Jihan el-Sadat. She had met Madam Sadat at the International Women's Year conference in Mexico in the summer of 1975.

Now, ten years later, Madam Sadat was a widow. Her husband, Egyptian President Anwar el-Sadat, had been assassinated in 1981. Madam Sadat had become a spokesperson for the expanding role of women in society and for world peace.

Madam Sadat agreed to come to Austin. Her topic was "The Road to Peace." In a gentle but persuasive voice, she emphasized the importance of people finding meaning in their lives by helping others.

During her visit, Madam Sadat was Liz's house guest at Grass Roots. To their delight, the women discovered they shared a love of the British poets.

The following year Jean M. Auel, author of *The Clan of the Cave Bear,* spoke on "Literature from Unlikely Places and Unlikely People."

"Funny Women: By Pen and Performance" was the theme for the third lectureship in 1987. Shana Alexander, Carol Channing, Nora Ephron, Fanny Flagg, Florence King, and Liz Smith talked about what humor is and what it does for us. Laughter from the audience often drowned out the speakers.

"Women are afraid to be funny," Florence King told the audience. "They're afraid of losing their femininity. Femininity is a defective characteristic. You're better off without it."

"Is Politics a Laughing Matter?" brought President Gerald Ford, television comedian Pat Paulsen, Mark Shields, and Jim Morris to Austin for the 1988 lectureship.

The following year "Word, Script, Image: The Art of Screenwriting" featured Jack Valenti, Marty Kaplan, Ernest Lehmann, prize-winning Texas playwright Horton Foote, and Jap Presson Allan.

Liz began to wonder if young women knew anything about the Women's Movement of the 1970s. A generation had grown up since the founding of the National Women's Political Caucus, the fight for ERA, and the early drives to get more women elected to office.

Wouldn't it be great, Liz thought, *to bring the "founding mothers" of the Women's Movement to Austin?* Liz invited Shana Alexander, Linda Ellerbee, Betty Friedan, Jill Ruckleshaus, and Sarah Weddington for a panel discussion.

"Calling All Women: To Celebrate Our Past and Embrace Our Future" was the 1991 lectureship. It was cosponsored by the Kozmetsky Centennial Lectureship and the Texas Union Distinguished Speakers Committee.

Wilhelmina Delco, Lena Guerrero, Kay Bailey Hutchison, and Jaqueline Trimier asked questions of the panel. The all-day session drew a crowd of nearly 3,000 and had to be moved to a larger auditorium.

Liz and the other participants were delighted with the eager response. The Women's Movement was far from dead. The young women who attended "Calling All Women" would be the leaders of today and tomorrow.

Betty Friedan was Liz's house guest. The two old friends talked into the night.

"I felt like the Movement had just been drifting for years," Betty Friedan said. "But all those cheering, vital women! It's given me a new spurt of energy."

Late at night the phone rang. It was for Betty. *Oh, dear,* Liz thought, *I hope it's not bad news for her.*

The wide smile on Betty's face relieved her fears. "Well," Betty said as she hung up the phone, "my daughter's in labor. I'm about to become a grandmother!"

The next year's lectureship was a complete change of pace: "Reaching Across the Species: Jane Goodall on Chimpanzees." Once again Liz was surprised and delighted at the large turnout. In her introductory remarks, Liz drew a humorous comparison between Jane Goodall's observation of chimps and her own lifelong study of politicians.

Liz went to the Democratic National Convention in New York in July 1992. This time she didn't go as a journalist, delegate, or campaign worker. As a lifelong Democrat, she just wanted to be a part of the excitement.

Bill Clinton won the party's nomination. Al Gore was selected as his running mate. Liz met Hillary Rodham Clinton. She gave Hillary some tips on whistlestop campaigning.

"After the election come on down to Texas," Liz added, already thinking ahead to the next lectureship. "Governor Ann Richards will be there, and Lady Bird Johnson. You'll have a great time."

Liz followed the campaign news closely. She admired the way Hillary Clinton and Tipper Gore spoke out on important issues as they campaigned for their husbands.

"These are the kinds of bright, articulate professional women this country needs," Liz told her friends.

A few years after Liz had moved to Grass Roots, Mrs. Johnson became one of her neighbors. When Mrs. Johnson came to visit, she often brought peaches from the Johnson Ranch or flowers from her garden. Liz went to Mrs. Johnson's home to swim or enjoy a light supper with her. The women continued the warm, easy friendship they had enjoyed for so many years.

As Mrs. Johnson's eightieth birthday neared, her family and friends asked Liz to help coordinate the event.

Fortunately, Liz didn't have to keep the celebration a secret. Mrs. Johnson had reluctantly given her permission. Her birthdate is December 22, but December 4, 1992, was selected for the dinner and dance at the LBJ Library.

Mrs. Johnson's daughters, Luci Johnson and Lynda Johnson Robb, were there, along with Mrs. Johnson's grandchildren. About 400 friends gathered to honor the former First Lady. Queen Elizabeth of England was among the many who sent birthday congratulations.

President Bill Clinton was inaugurated January 20, 1993. Hillary began work as head of the new Task Force on National Health Care Reform. Not since FDR appointed Eleanor Roosevelt as codirector of the Office for Civil Defense had a First Lady held a post in her husband's administration.

The Eighth Annual Liz Sutherland Carpenter Lectureship was scheduled for April 6. Time grew near for Hillary Clinton to come to Austin. Mrs. Clinton's father, Hugh Rodham, suffered a stroke March 19. She flew from Washington to Little Rock to be near him. He seemed to improve.

In Austin, plans went ahead for Mrs. Clinton's visit to the Frank Erwin Center on the university campus.

Liz, Mrs. Clinton, Mrs. Johnson, and Ann Richards, with about twenty of the other participants, had a luncheon in the Green Room of the Erwin Center. Mrs. Clinton listened carefully to what each person had to say.

"In July 1971 we formed the National Women's Political Caucus," Liz told the audience in her introduction. "We wanted to urge women to run for public office and sometimes win."

Liz wore a scarf of burnt orange and white — University of Texas colors. She carried a burnt orange walking stick decorated by her childhood friend, Sue Kone Drake.

"What was that noisy, pushy movement all about?" Liz continued. "It was about a housewife from Waco, mother of four, with a lot of political savvy, who's now our

Texas governor. It's about a law student who took honors at Yale and now leads us as First Lady.

"Mrs. Clinton's topic is 'Remolding Our Society,'" Liz said. "God knows we need it." Liz left the podium. She sat next to Mrs. Johnson in the audience.

Governor Ann Richards paid tribute to Liz. "I don't say this often enough. I want to say it now. Thank God for Liz Carpenter and for the effect and influence she has had on all our lives."

Mrs. Johnson leaned toward Liz and touched her fingertips to her friend's shoulder. "We're all so proud of you," she whispered. Liz fought back tears.

"When Liz invited me to come to Austin," Hillary Clinton told the audience, "I expected a small seminar room in the LBJ Library with Governor Richards and Mrs. Johnson and maybe a few students. I didn't expect fourteen thousand people. I know now you can't question Liz. If she has a lecture, it will be a big one. And besides, this is Texas."

Mrs. Clinton paid tribute to Mrs. Johnson. "Until you've walked in the other person's moccasins, you can't know what it's like, as First Lady, to try to balance your family life and your public life."

In Mrs. Clinton's forty-five-minute talk, it was obvious she had listened well to the comments at the luncheon. She touched on many of the concerns the others had mentioned.

A panel discussion followed Mrs. Clinton's talk. Sarah Weddington, Mary Beth Rogers, Barbara White, Paul Leong, and Ronnye Vargas were panel members.

Liz's friend of many years, Bill Moyers, was the panel moderator. In his closing remarks he paid tribute to Liz, "who took me to my first press conference in Washington when I was a skinny kid just out of the university with my journalism degree."

He reminded the audience of the number of celebrities and gifted speakers Liz had brought to Austin.

"The Liz Sutherland Carpenter Distinguished Lectureship," Moyers concluded, "is the modern day equivalent of the old-time Chautaugua, Constitution Hall in Washington, and Mrs. Sutherland's dining table in Salado."

Afterword

Liz's brother, Tommy Sutherland, died September 14, 1991. He was just a week short of his eightieth birthday.

During his long illness he talked earnestly to Liz about his young children. He had three minor children from his second marriage: Tommy (Thomas Shelton Sutherland V), young Liz (Nancy Elizabeth Sutherland), and Mary (Mary Robertson Sutherland).

After her brother's death, Liz opened her heart and her home to his youngsters. She had promised Tommy she would. With little time for dealing with her own grief, she plunged into getting the children's school records transferred, helping them register, attending PTA for the first time in decades, packing lunches, delivering to and picking up from three separate schools, and juggling the children's piano lessons and soccer schedules between her own speaking engagements.

"When I shopped for groceries for a houseful of hungry teenagers, I was scared to look at the checkout stand tabloids," she said. "I was afraid I'd see a headline, **Liz Carpenter Becomes Mother of Three at 71.**"

Liz began jotting down some of the more humorous anecdotes of late motherhood to use in her speeches. She soon realized her situation was not unique. Many older men and women, she discovered, suddenly find themselves raising their grandchildren or young nieces and nephews. She began writing a book, *Unplanned Parenthood,* based on her experiences.

Liz discovered that she could walk more easily with the aid of a cane or walking stick. Beside her front door at Grass Roots, an umbrella stand holds a dozen of them. Sue Kone Drake, Liz's friend since the second grade, decorated them. They range from bandanna red to burnt orange to black velvet with sequins. Liz has only to select one to match the occasion to step out in style. And no one can do that better than the girl from Salado, Liz Carpenter.

Liz now finds that she walks more easily with the help of a cane. She is shown here with Carol Channing. Standing beside Carol is Liz's step-granddaughter, Bonnie Bizzell.

The GBATTS (Getting Better All the Time) have grown from informal singing and poetry readings to costumed and choreographed performances before large audiences. The BGATT performers: Sarah Jane English, Mary Denman (guest), Fred Ward, Henrietta Jacobsen, Christian Smith, Liz Carpenter, Dick Hardin, Coleen Hardin, Ken Koock, Lael Seagert, George Seagert, and Martha Deatherage.

Glossary

Air Force One — the name for any aircraft normally reserved for the use of the president of the United States.
antebellum — existing before the Civil War.
ancestor — a forefather, or one from whom a person is descended.
ancestry — one's early family or line of descent.
anesthetic — a substance that helps control pain.
appendectomy — the surgical removal of the appendix.
arborvitae — an evergreen tree.
asphalt — a dark-colored, tarlike substance used for paving streets and roads.
assassination — a politically motivated killing.
auxiliary — a reserve or voluntary group called on in an emergency.
bankrupt — having no money; unable to pay debts.
bay horse — a reddish-brown horse, often with black mane and tail.
beat — the news or activity a reporter is assigned to cover.
belle — a woman admired for her beauty and charm.
blacklist — a list of persons under suspicion who are not to be hired or admitted to membership.
blackout — all visible lights hidden to protect against air raids.
bootleg — to make or sell illegal alcoholic beverages.
byline — line under the headline or title of a printed work giving the author's name.
cabinet — high-level advisers to the president, sometimes called the "president's official family"; each has responsibility for a certain area, such as defense, labor, treasury, etc.

cadence — the rhythmic flow of sounds or words.
calling cards — social or visiting cards, similar to business cards.
campaign — a series of activities designed to elect a person to office.
cantankerous — quarrelsome or irritable.
caucus — a meeting of members of a political group.
chair — a position of authority or dignity, especially an endowed position with a university.
choreography — an arrangement of dance steps.
clan — a group of families descended from a common ancestor.
cloudburst — a sudden and very heavy rainfall.
cold war — term used to describe distrust and suspicion between the United States and the Soviet Union following World War II.
collaborate — to work with another person to write a play, story, or song.
colony — a group of people who leave their native country to form settlements in a new land.
comtometer — key-driven accounting and calculating machine.
condolences — expressions of sympathy.
conductor — person in charge of a train.
constituents — voters in a district represented by an elected official.
convalesce — to get well after an illness.
cotton boll — the rounded seedpod of cotton.
cotton gin — a machine for separating cotton fiber from the seeds.
cutline — a caption (written description) appearing beneath a photograph in a newspaper or magazine.
depression — a period of hard economic times and widespread unemployment.
drought — an extended period of dry weather.
"dry" — a person who favors laws against the sale of alcoholic beverages.
empresario — (em pre SAH rio) Spanish word for a person who enters into a contract to bring in colonists.
endow — to provide a fund of money or a source of income.
ensign — a commissioned officer in the Navy or Coast Guard.
ether — formerly used as an inhalant to control pain.
extra — a special edition of a newspaper.

feature stories — articles about people or events, written with a personal slant.
firmament — the sky.
foreman — person in charge of a group of workers.
freelance — a person, such as a writer, who sells work or services without working for a regular salary.
galluses — suspenders for pants or trousers.
grassroots — ordinary people in a political, social, or economic group.
green room — a lounge or waiting room for performers when they are not on stage.
highwayman — a holdup man who robbed travelers along a public road.
hydrophobia — "fear of water"; another name for rabies.
impeachment — a way of removing officials from office before their term expires. The House of Representatives may bring charges of impeachment. The Senate then acts as a court to hear the case. A two-thirds vote is necessary for conviction. Impeachment charges were brought against President Andrew Johnson in 1868. President Johnson was tried in the Senate but was not convicted. He remained in office until his term expired.
"in the red" — an expression meaning "out of money."
Inauguration Day — The day the president takes the oath of office. Changed (in 1937) from March 4 to January 20.
infamy — reputation based on an extremely bad, shameful, or criminal act.
interurban — a transportation system operating between two cities.
jaunty — nonchalant, carefree.
journalist — a writer for a newspaper or magazine.
keynote speech — at a political convention, an address that sets the tone and outlines the goals of the convention.
lariat — a loop or rope used to catch livestock.
lectern — a reading desk for a standing reader or speaker.
majority — in election returns, a number of votes greater than half the total.
media — mass communications, such as newspapers, magazines, the news services, radio, and television.
mesquite — spiny bushes or trees with beanlike pods and often forming dense thickets.

militia — a body of citizens called into active service in times of emergency.

missal — a priest's book of prayers and rites.

motorcade — a procession of motor vehicles.

nib — penpoint.

oration — a formal public speech.

page — (noun) someone employed to deliver messages or run errands; (verb) to summon by calling out someone's name.

pallet — a small or makeshift bed.

parliamentarian — an officer of a legislative body; an expert on rules of order.

Pasteur Institute — a medical treatment center named for the French scientist Louis Pasteur.

plantation — a large farm or estate.

platform — statement of goals and principles of a political party.

plurality — in an election among three or more candidates, the excess of votes for the winning candidate over the next candidate.

podium — a raised platform for a speaker or performer.

pool reporter — a small group of reporters, each chosen to represent her or his news service.

press kit — packet of information on a particular subject that is given to the media, particularly at a press conference.

prohibition — laws against manufacture, sale, and transportation of alcoholic beverages.

prosperity — economic good times.

"put to bed" — make final preparations for printing a newspaper or magazine.

quarantine — isolation to prevent the spread of infectious diseases.

quip — a clever or witty remark.

rabies — a fatal disease of dogs, cats, and sometimes people.

ragtag — ragged or shabby; made up of mixed elements.

ratify — to express approval or consent.

ration coupons — tickets or stamps exchanged for scarce food or goods.

rationing — restricting amounts of scarce food or goods that may be bought or sold.

repertoire — all the works a performing group is prepared to present.

running mate — a candidate for political office linked with a candidate for a higher office.
rural — living in the country.
ruse — a trick intended to deceive.
salutatorian — second highest-ranking student in a graduating class.
satirist — a person who writes or otherwise uses satire (wit or irony used to attack or make fun of persons or literary works).
settlement — a colony; a small community or village.
sidebar — a short news feature highlighting a longer story.
slot — the position of the copy editor on the inside of a horseshoe-shaped copy desk in a newspaper office.
sob sister — a journalist who writes overly sentimental feature stories.
solicitor — one who seeks trade or contributions; in England, term used for lawyer.
sorority — a group of girls or women, especially in college or in a profession.
stockman — a person who owns or raises livestock.
straight ticket — ballot cast for all the candidates of one political party.
stumping — making political speeches.
suffrage — the right to vote.
suffragist — one who favors the right to vote, especially for women.
Tin Lizzie — a cheap, old car.
tornado — a violent, destructive windstorm.
trestles — the framework supporting bridges.
trolley car — a streetcar run by electricity from overhead wires and cables.
twister — a whirlwind or tornado.
vaccine — a substance used to prevent a disease.
vaquero — (vah KAY row) Spanish word for cowboys or herdsmen.
watercress — plant that grows in clear, running streams.
wattle — a fleshy flap of skin hanging from a turkey's throat.
"wet" — a person who favors legal sale of alcoholic beverages.
whistlestop — a brief personal appearance by a political candidate; a short political talk from the rear platform of a train.
zeal — enthusiasm; dedication to a goal or cause.

Bibliography

Books:

Allen, Frederick Lewis. *Only Yesterday.* New York: Bantam Books, 1952.

Angle, Paul M. *The American Reader.* New York: Rand McNally, 1958.

Austin High School. Publications Department. *100 Years of Education: The Centennial History of Austin High School.* 1980.

Austin Institute of Architects. Austin chapter. *Austin: Its Architect and Architecture (1836–1986).* Austin: 1986.

Banks, Jimmy. *Money, Marbles and Chalk.* Austin: Texas Pub. Co., 1971.

Barkley, Mary Starr. *History of Travis County and Austin, 1839–1899.* Waco: Texian Press, 1963.

Beasley, Maurine. *The White House Press Conferences of Eleanor Roosevelt.* New York: Garland Publishing, Inc., 1983.

———, and Sheila Silver. *Women in Media.* Washington, D.C.: Women's Institute for Freedom of the Press, 1977.

Bell County Historical Commission. *Story of Bell County, Texas.* Vols. I and II. Austin: Eakin Press, 1988.

Brown, Norman D. *Hood, Bonnet, and Little Brown Jug. Texas Politics, 1921–1928.* College Station: Texas A&M Press, 1983.

Burns, James MacGregor. *Roosevelt: The Soldier of Freedom.* New York: Harcourt Brace Jovanovich, 1971.

Carpenter, Liz. *Getting Better All the Time.* New York: Simon & Schuster, 1987.

———. *Ruffles and Flourishes.* New York: Doubleday & Company, 1970.

Chronicle of America. Mount Kisco, N.Y.: Chronicle Publications, n.d.

Cox, Mike. *Texas Rangers: Men of Action and Valor.* Austin: Eakin Press, 1991.

Crawford, Ann Fears, and Crystal Sasse Ragsdale. *Women in Texas.* Austin: State House Press, 1992.

Dallas Morning News. *November 22 — The Day Remembered.* Dallas: Taylor Publishing Co., 1990.

Dallek, Robert. *Lone Star Rising: Lyndon Johnson and His Times, 1908–1960.* New York: Oxford University Press, 1991.

Daniel, Jean Houston, Price Daniel, and Dorothy Blodgett. *The Texas Governor's Mansion.* Austin: Texas State Library and Archives, 1984.

Davis, Flora. *Moving the Mountain: The Women's Movement in America Since 1950.* New York: Simon & Schuster, 1991.

Fehrenbach, T. R. *Lone Star: A History of Texas and the Texans.* New York: Macmillan, 1968.

Flynn, Jean. *Lady: The Story of Claudia Alta (Lady Bird) Johnson, Texas' First Lady.* Austin: Eakin Press, 1991.

Ford, Betty, and Chris Chase. *The Times of My Life.* New York: Harper & Row, 1978.

Friends of the Governor's Mansion. *The Governor's Mansion of Texas: A Historic Tour.* Austin: 1985.

Gould, Lewis L. *Lady Bird Johnson and the Environment.* Lawrence: University Press of Kansas, 1988.

Handbook of Texas. Vols. I and II. Austin: Texas State Historical Association, 1952. Vol. III. Austin: Texas State Historical Association, 1976.

Harllee, William Curry. *Kinfolks.* Vol. III. New Orleans: Searcy & Pfaff, 1937.

Harris County Historical Society, Inc., sponsor. *Houston, A History and Guide.* Houston: Anson Jones Press, 1942.

Humphrey, David C., and Betty Wilke Hudman. *Austin: An Illustrated History.* Woodland Hills, CA: Windsor, 1985.

Johnson, Claudia Alta (Taylor). *White House Diary.* New York: Holt, Rinehart and Winston, 1970.

Johnson, Lyndon Baines. *The Vantage Point: Perspectives of the President, 1963–1969.* New York: Holt, Rinehart and Winston, 1971.

Lasher, Patricia. *Texas Women, Interviews and Images.* Austin: Shoal Creek, 1980.
Miller, Merle. *Lyndon: An Oral Biography.* New York: G. P. Putnam's Sons, 1980.
Read, Phyllis J., and Bernard L. Witlieb. *The Book of Women's Firsts.* New York: Random House, 1992.
Richards, Ann, with Peter Knobler. *Straight from the Heart.* New York: Simon & Schuster, 1989.
Rogers, Mary Beth. *Texas Women, A Celebration of History.* Texas Foundation for Women's Resources, 1981.
Scharf, Lois. *Eleanor Roosevelt, First Lady of American Liberalism.* Boston: Twayne, 1987.
Shanklin, Felda Davis. *Salado, Texas.* Belton: Peter Hansbrough Bell Press, 1960.
Texas. University. Department of Public Relations. *A University Goes to War.* Austin: University of Texas Press, April 1942.
Tyler, George W. *The History of Bell County.* San Antonio: Naylor, 1930.
WPA. *Texas: A Guide to the Lone Star State.* New York: Hastings House, 1940.

Unpublished material:

Hudson, Florence Sutherland, comp. "We Cousins, Virginia to Texas." Unpublished typescript. San Benito, TX: 1957.
Sutherland, Kay. "Gone with Gypsy Time: Conversations with a Texas Poet and Storyteller." Unpublished manuscript based on oral recollections of Tommy Sutherland (Thomas Shelton Sutherland IV, 1911–1991).

Newspapers, magazines, and serials:

Alcalde
Austin American
Austin Statesman
Austin American-Statesman
Cactus (University of Texas yearbook)
Comet (Austin High School yearbook)
Daily Texan
Dallas Morning News
Dallas Times Herald

Family Circle
Fort Worth Star Telegram
Houston Chronicle
New York Times
People
Parade
Texas Almanac
Ultra
UTmost
Washington Post
Washington Star

McBee, Sue Brandt. "An Evening on Liz's Hilltop." *Austin Homes and Gardens,* March 1980.

Index

I

J

K

L

T